EMOTIONAL INTELLIGENCE
DEVELOP EXTRAORDINARY RELATIONSHIPS, PEOPLE SKILLS, AND SOCIAL SKILLS

THERESA CHANG

CONTENTS

Introduction   v

1. Meaning of Emotional Intelligence   1
2. Tips for Improving Emotional Intelligence   8
3. Ways to Develop Your Self-Awareness   15
4. Strategies for Increasing Self-Control   22
5. Strategies for Increasing Motivation   29
6. Ways to Improve Empathy   36
7. Ways to Develop Social Skills   43
8. How Emotional Intelligence Improves Your Life   50
9. How to Practice Gratitude   56
10. Techniques for Developing Patience   62
11. Methods of Boosting Creativity   68
12. Tips for Building Curiosity   75
13. Tips for Mastering Your Emotions   82
14. Careers for People with High Emotional Intelligence   89
15. Habits of Emotionally Healthy People   95
16. Ways of Developing a Positive Mindset   102
17. How to increase your willpower   109
18. How to stop being lazy   114
19. Emotional Intelligence in Leadership   122
20. Emotional Intelligence FAQ   130

Copyright © 2019 by Theresa Chang

All rights reserved.

No part of this book may be reproduced in any form or by any electronic or mechanical means, including information storage and retrieval systems, without written permission from the author, except for the use of brief quotations in a book review.

INTRODUCTION

You can be the best of your kind in any domain, but if you lack the capacity to connect with people, your visibility will be unfairly small. For success to take place, people must be in the equation, and it doesn't matter the nature of your business. However, in order to draw people's attention to your business, you have to be able to connect with them emotionally. You can achieve this by developing a skill known as emotional intelligence. It basically refers to an individual's capacity to be in control of their emotions and to be great at interpersonal relationships. Someone with a high emotional intelligence has a massive head start, and they are likely to reach their goals. This book caters to the subject of emotional intelligence, shining a light on the various components of this skill that ought to be developed, so that one may lead a fulfilling life. Some of the topics explored include:

- Self-awareness
- Self-regulation

INTRODUCTION

- Social skills
- Empathy

MEANING OF EMOTIONAL INTELLIGENCE

When we say that someone is emotionally intelligent, this is precisely what we mean: that this person is in control of their emotions, can perceive a range of emotions, and can monitor the emotional statues of other people. They are well aware of how various emotions can affect their lives. Emotions have a great impact on our life journeys as they inform every decision we make.

For the longest time, people have thought that intelligent quotient (IQ) is the most important factor in success, but research has shown that emotional quotient (EQ) is just as important, if not more important than IQ. And the reason is simple. IQ merely helps you to acquire knowledge, but EQ helps you connect with human beings, who are the gatekeepers of success. A person with a high EQ but an average IQ stands a far greater chance at succeeding than a person with a low EQ but a high IQ.

Emotional intelligence is made up of four main branches, namely: self-awareness, self-management, social awareness, and relationship management.

But how would you tell that you – or someone else – are emotionally intelligent? What are the signs that indicate emotional intelligence?

- **They permit themselves to experience various emotions**

One of the reasons that there's so much pain in the world is because people tend to overestimate their resilience and block out their emotions. Successful people understand there's no shame in "feeling" their negative emotions because that's the easiest way of getting away from them. Once you have experienced these emotions, which are usually the mind's way of passing a message across, now you can focus on the healing process. On the other hand, when you suppress your feelings, you are sucked into a black hole of negativity, and it becomes increasingly hard for you to be productive. Emotionally intelligent people are into experiencing the full range of their emotions.

- **They are capable of assessing themselves**

This is an extremely important skill because it's a major factor in every decision you make. An individual's self-assess capacity is what determines whether they'll be realistic or come across as deluded. An emotionally intelligent person has taken the time to study their strengths and weaknesses. This enables them to align themselves with the course of events that will elevate them. On the other hand, someone lacking in self-assessment skill will likely be a chance taker. They will sail whichever side the wind carries them. And such an attitude denies them the capacity to formulate goals and work toward success.

- **They are self-confident**

Part of the reason why emotionally intelligent people have self-confidence is that they understand that imperfections are to be embraced, celebrated even, and not something to be ashamed about. A person who treats their imperfections as liabilities is bound to have a lot of trouble in life. This is simply because no one is perfect. If you are scared of someone else judging you, understand that everyone else is just as scared. When you view your imperfections as liabilities, you are likely to develop self-inhibiting habits that will stop you from living life to the full. But emotionally intelligent people have an awesome life thanks to their self-confidence.

- **They can control their emotions**

When a dog gets mad, she's likely to fight the source of her fear. We may think that this behavior is exclusive to animals, but even some human beings have similar tendencies. But that's not how it should be. A human being should harbor rational thought that compels him or her to consider both the pros and cons of taking a particular decision. An emotionally intelligent person embodies this type of human. She can be mad at her spouse but still express her disappointment in an even tone; she can be frustrated with your colleagues but still let them know their errors calmly. If you are used to emotional outbursts, it can be a bit hard to cultivate such a mentality, but it really helps in the long run.

- **They achieve success**

This is not to mean that every emotionally intelligent person is a millionaire. There are other factors besides emotional intelligence that determine whether a person will be successful or not. But then emotionally intelligent people are goal-driven. They have put down both short term and long term goals that they are working towards. Also, their self-confidence makes them unbowed as they fight to wade through their challenges and come out at the top. Emotionally intelligent people don't treat success as one shot, but rather, they conceive success as a journey. Thus, instead of looking for a golden bullet, they prefer creating lifestyles that breed success. Emotionally intelligent people are persistent in their endeavors, and "failure" doesn't slow them down or cause them to lose all hope.

- **They are self-driven**

One of the biggest problems that people have is an inability to take the initiative. They imagine that it is someone else's business to take care of a particular thing when it's squarely up to them or it doesn't happen. For instance, if you are a new talent in the writing industry, you obviously need a mentor so you may quicken your success. But then you have to take the initiative to approach various established writers for a chance to work with them, because if you don't reach out to them they are unlikely to reach out to you first, and you'll lose out. Emotionally intelligent people understand the need for being proactive, and they always make decisions that help them move ahead in life.

- **They are honest**

Honesty is an individual's capacity to be transparent about their motives. It is an extremely rare virtue. But then it can be found in emotionally intelligent people. Thus, we can infer that the number of emotionally intelligent people in this world is on the low side. Considering that honesty is a rare thing, those who have it become huge assets in society. It causes more people to take a liking to you. Is there a guarantee that all emotionally intelligent people are honest? By no means! But, then, someone with sufficient emotional intelligence is likely to be honest.

- **They are grateful**

If you see someone who never appreciates people's contributions, you can be sure of one thing; they are not emotionally intelligent. An emotionally intelligent person is bound to appreciate other people for the role that they play in improving their life. If gratitude is your virtue, you will not be grateful for the big things that happen in your life but also for the small things. People who are grateful, never forget to acknowledge the people that helped them scale the heights of success.

- **They are not stuck in the past**

There are many people with amazing potential that hardly ever make progress. One of the reasons could be that they are stuck in the past. Such people have a victim mentality and a distorted perception of the world. Evidently, they have poor emotional intelligence. People with high emotional intelligence tend to move on from their ugly past. They have hope for tomorrow, and this keeps them stretching the limits. One the victim mentality creeps up on a person it denies them the courage to pursue their goals.

- **They have boundaries**

Emotionally intelligent people are well aware that friends, acquaintances, and even family can easily drain their time and energy and effectively slow them down. Emotionally intelligent people create boundaries so as to protect their interests. They are aware that their intentions may be misinterpreted, but still, it doesn't keep them from establishing boundaries. If a person lacks boundaries, they are unlikely to muster the discipline required to continue showing up for the realization of their goals. A lack of boundaries signifies a lack of direction, and it is a major negative issue.

- **They provide solutions**

At the end of the day, success is about coming up with a solution. In some way, success can be measured in terms of the number of people affected by a particular solution, and that may be precisely why, billionaires create global-targeted solutions, and millionaires target fewer demographics in comparison. Before you can come up with a solution, you need to first understand the problem, yet in a multi-layered manner. You need to understand precisely how things will turn out after your solution is applied. And this is definitely not an exercise that a person lacking in emotional intelligence would undertake.

- **They have a good attitude**

Most people have a bad attitude, and needless to say, they even get hurt by words and actions that weren't meant to hurt them. In some instances, their bad attitude can be attributed to their low emotional intelligence. People with high emotional intelligence have a great attitude. And this trait of theirs makes them popular among people. Thanks to their easygoing nature, most people feel comfortable around them, and this allows them to leverage their influence. A good attitude is such an underrated quality in an individual.

TIPS FOR IMPROVING EMOTIONAL INTELLIGENCE

Emotional intelligence is not ingrained in our DNA. This means it can be developed as long as one applies the effort. Having high emotional intelligence helps you live abundantly. You get to minimize errors from your decisions, and at the same time, you take maximum advantage of opportunities. These factors enhance your prospect of attaining success. Use the following tips to increase your emotional intelligence.

- **Rid yourself of stress**

One of the factors that hold people back from increasing their emotional intelligence is stress. People collect stress by virtue of both their actions and inactions. But when you learn to relieve yourself of stress, you get into the right mindset of developing emotional intelligence. There are many stress reduction techniques, but whether they work, it depends from person to person. While some people might fight away their stress through running, others will need to take time off, and be alone, and then the stress will go away. So, it is upon you to find the technique that works in eliminating stress from your life.

- **Stop judging**

Human beings tend to be very judgmental. Sometimes it might come to us unconsciously, fuelled by our deepest convictions. For instance, if you hold that people of a particular race are violent robbers, next time a person from that race gets close to you, you may instinctively hold your possessions tighter. You judged them. Being a judgmental person will stifle your capacity to develop emotional intelligence. Thus, you have to see to it that you are fighting away this tendency. Start by practicing critical thinking and realizing that a person's behavior is not necessarily influenced by things such as race or religion.

- **Be kinder**

We live in a broken world. If you want to see how broken the world is. Just tune to your favorite international news channel, and you'll see for yourself. Where's humanity? Some of the news items are so atrocious you would think it's an animal – not a human being – behind the injustice. The only way to right this wrong is through being kind on purpose. Ensure that you are spreading the vibe of kindness wherever you are, and you may just inspire someone else to be as kind as you. Studies show that kindness helps an individual experience pleasure in their mind. So, by being kind, you get to assist someone, and you also feel great about yourself. But more importantly, kindness helps build your emotional intelligence.

- **Quit taking rush decisions**

One of the ways that people stifle their emotional intelligence is through making impulsive decisions. This means they hardly ever sit down to think through their actions. You should learn to "sit with your emotions." For instance, if you receive some terrible news, and you are consumed with anger, instead of picking up the phone and calling someone you believed has wronged you to vent at them, just sit down and listen to your emotions. The more you can take an observer's role over your emotions, the more you get to understand yourself. And such an attitude contributes to the expansion of your emotional intelligence.

- **Learn to accept criticism**

If you just sit around and do nothing people will criticize you. You are damned if you do, and you are damned if you don't. So, how about being criticized for at least doing something? Being able to take criticism with no ill feelings is not something that happens overnight, but it is an incredibly important step. It toughens you up. You will need to be emotionally tough before you can ever make your dreams come true. Constructive criticism actually is aimed at building you up. You just need to take note of the important things that have been mentioned. But then you have to prepare yourself to handle negative criticism. Most of the times, negative criticism is not about you, but it's about them, as such critics get off on bullying other people. In other words, they have low self-esteem and are actually deserving of pity.

- **Know your weaknesses**

Thinking that you have no weaknesses reeks of pride. The fact is, you have some weaknesses, and maybe your inability to recognize these weaknesses is a weakness in itself. A person who's well aware of their weak spots will choose their battles pretty well. And they are also great aligning themselves for success. In order to recognize your weaknesses, you have to spend time with yourself and analyze various aspects of your life. By gaining knowledge about yourself, you increase your capacity to understand other human beings.

- **Become an active listener**

Studies show that the easiest way to promote understanding between parties is through active listening. This involves listening to your partner with rapt attention. It shows that you value their contribution and that you are interested in developing the conversation. Being an active listener will increase your capacity to respect other people, and also, it will boost your emotional intelligence.

- **Apologize**

Most awesome relationships tumble down simply because one or both parties have trouble apologizing. It is rooted in their misconception that apologizing makes them look small or weak. Actually, being able to apologize is indicative of strength. You want to be the sort of person that acknowledges their wrongs and asks the other person to pardon them. But then apologizing is not enough, you need back it up with proof of behavior modification.

- **Give others a chance to talk**

Yes, you may have a high IQ and all, but you don't quite know everything there is to know on this earth. That's why it's important to give other people a chance to talk. Such an attitude encourages the flow of information which promotes creativity. But even better than that, such an attitude promotes your capacity to relate well with other people, and by extension, your emotional health.

- **Learn to express your negative emotions**

You can never run away from negative emotions. There's an overabundance of negativity. But then you can choose how you label these emotions. Take some time to think through these negative emotions and express them in the calmest manner. This will help you have your emotions in check. If you have a tendency of expressing your negative emotions in an abrupt manner, you will stifle your chance of developing emotional intelligence, and also gain a bad reputation.

- **Think deeply before you decide to accept a belief**

Every person has a belief that has taken deep root. But the question is, how did they acquire this belief? If it was through indoctrination, then that's a big red flag. A person should develop beliefs after thinking them through. For instance, if you want to decide over your religious standing, you might want to think critically about various holy texts and reconcile them with the facts of modern religion and seek to find the truth. In the end, you will make a conclusion basing on the evidence that you found. Learn to think critically for yourself.

- **Learn to say, "No."**

Many people have a hard time saying "No" because they imagine it upsets the next person. But saying "No" when you mean it actually wins you some respect. It shows that you are not a pushover. It causes people to respect your opinions and your stand. If you are not used to saying that, it can feel a bit uncomfortable, but once you have done it enough times, you will become comfortable. This ability frees you up from unnecessary demands and helps you live your best life. If you are too scared to tell people that you cannot meet their expectations, you will needlessly overburden yourself, make your life unpleasant, and develop negative emotions.

- **Acknowledge what other people are feeling**

Another secret of developing emotional intelligence is to acknowledge what other people are feeling. If you are good at reading people, you should be able to tell what they must be feeling from just looking at their facial expressions and body language. This gives you a chance to show them empathy. Acknowledging what other people are feeling also helps you to create a bond with them, and it also helps you register the various ways you can help people.

- **Become a trustworthy person**

It's not easy to acquire the reputation of being a trustworthy person. This is simply because most people are guarded. They don't want to rely on another person because, probably, experience has taught them otherwise. Very rarely will you share a secret with someone and they will honor their promise of secrecy. But if you can manage to convince people that you are a trustworthy person, it promotes your emotional health. If people trust you, they will always cooperate with you. One of the best ways you can in the trust of many people is through working toward an objective that is close to their hearts.

WAYS TO DEVELOP YOUR SELF-AWARENESS

Self-awareness is an individual's capacity to fully understand oneself and also recognize how others perceive them. Someone with a high level of self-awareness understands his personality, knows his strengths and weaknesses, beliefs, motivations, and fears. Being self-aware is essential as it keeps you grounded. An individual who lacks self-awareness skills is likely to be carried away by fantasies of their limitless potential, causing them to take unbecoming decisions, which could hinder them from realizing their potential.

Benefits of self-awareness:

1. Promotes rationality: for a person lacking in self-awareness, they may react instinctively to various people and things, which can lead to nasty results. But when someone develops self-awareness, they are in a position to think through the effects of their actions, and this puts them at less risk.

2. Self-love: in the modern world, it's so easy to hate your life and consider yourself a loser. The fact that social media enables our desire to compete against the world doesn't help matters. It's hard to be proud of yourself when everyone but you appears to be living their dream. But then, through self-awareness, you can learn to separate yourself from the expectations of the world, to live on your own terms, aiming for your goals and paying no attention to distractions. You can learn to be happy in your own skin.

3. Happiness: everyone is in the business of looking for happiness. Some people hold the misleading notion that happiness can be found in material possessions. But when they acquire more material, it leaves them even emptier. True happiness is about appreciating what you are, making peace with your weaknesses, and realizing that you are enough.

4. Improved quality of life: being self-aware is all about increasing your understanding of self. And when you understand yourself at a deep level, you are in a position to know the things that make you truly happy and seek them. This makes your life sweet and interesting.

5. Banish negativity: no matter where you are or what you're doing, it's hard to escape negative energy. This is primarily because people are mostly negative. But when you develop your self-awareness, you'll be in a position to resist negative energy and focus on the bright side.

6. Being real: one of the problems most people have is being inauthentic. There are so many people who try to be what they are not. They end up looking ridiculous. But through self-awareness, a person gets to understand that it's okay to express their true self and stand out.

7. Courageous living: when you increase your level of self-awareness, you also become much bolder and courageous. You are not afraid anymore of making unpopular decisions as long as they serve your purpose. Courage is a necessary quality for success.

8. Better relationships: human beings are social beings. We must form personal, business, and career relationships in order to thrive. People with limited ability to form relationships with others have it tough. The more you become self-aware, the higher your chances of starting healthy relationships.

How to develop your self-awareness:

The following are some of the vital techniques that will help you increase your level of self-awareness:

- **Recognize your strengths and weaknesses**

Some people seem to think of themselves as gods or goddesses among mortals. That's a deceptive mentality. As a human being, you must realize you are imperfect. It starts by questioning your strengths and weaknesses. What are you good at? And what are you terrible at? The more you get to learn of your various capabilities, the wiser you become, and it orients you in the direction of success.

- **Actively seek feedback**

Many of our habits and thoughts may escape our attention because of our bias. In other words, we may develop bad habits and not even realize it. But the remedy is actually to let people point it out.

Of course, being criticized is not akin to lying on a bed of roses. But people look at you from different angles, and they can notice your apparent shortcomings. Learn to take the criticism that comes your way and make an effort to become a better person.

- **Embrace your intuition**

The gift of intuition is very much like any other gift: if you don't use it, you may lose it. Start watering this gift so that you can raise your levels of self-awareness. First off, understand that intuition helps you perceive other people's motives. Spare some minutes every day to indulge in exercises that will strengthen your intuitive gifts. Also, try to put yourself out there more, so that you may have a chance to exercise your gifts. Once you have a thorough understanding of both yourself and the world around you, you'll be well on your way toward living a responsible and fruitful life.

- **Understand your emotional triggers**

An emotional trigger is an event that causes you to experience a particular emotion. For instance, if you were once involved in a road accident, it was an obviously traumatizing event. Any moment you think back to that accident, you are filled up with sorrow. Thus, that accident is an emotional trigger. So, make a list of all the events and situations that cause you to feel a certain way. Emotions play a key role in the wellbeing of an individual. Thus, understanding your emotions is a giant leap forward. It will increase your level of self-awareness.

- **Establish boundaries**

Setting boundaries doesn't mean you are a "terrible" person, but rather, it is a way of protecting your interests, which is what any sane person should do. It is not a crime to be ambitious. Boundaries exist so that other people can know there's a limit to how they may interact with you. For instance, if you are in the consultation industry, and you have most clients in the morning hours, you may decline to answer non-business calls or emails within that time. Learning to prioritize your goals helps you discover the fighting spirit within you. When you set goals, expect that people will disregard them. Thus, you have to have a punishment ready.

- **Increase your self-control**

Unless we have self-control, in other words, discipline, we can barely make progress in life. At any given time, there are various things competing for our attention. Sometimes our own passions might blind us to what is objectively more important. For instance, if you have an insatiable sexual appetite, you may give in to your temptations and end up spending more money on sex at the expense of your family. Self-control helps you realize what is important in life and fight for it whilst you ignore distractions.

- **Have an open mind**

We live in a vast world. Actually, wouldn't it be boring if every last one of us held the same viewpoint? Having an open mind means that you are welcoming of even those you don't agree with. It means you can listen to other people that hold contrary beliefs, and if you find any truth to their arguments, you'll be more than ready to believe as they do. Having an open mind allows you to consume a lot of information, and it helps you become creative.

- **Get out of your comfort zone**

Most people hate the idea of struggle. They want to stay in their comfort zone as long as they can meet their basic needs and afford few luxuries. But staying in the comfort zone hinders personal development. It denies you the chance to know what you are capable of. Even ambitious people can be so easily trapped in living in their comfort zone. After every milestone or goal you achieve, set your sights on the next major challenge, as opposed to basking in your glory for an extended period. Challenging yourself on a constant basis helps you realize how strong you are.

- **Motivate yourself**

Some people are so talented, but they never succeed because they never motivate themselves. They only act when they feel inspired. Such a mentality can hinder you from understanding what you truly are. Motivating yourself means that you'll adhere to your schedule no matter what goes down. On many occasions, you'll find yourself wanting to look for reasons to avid work, simply because you lack the motivation. But then you must motivate yourself and work anyway. When you are used to motivating yourself, you become much more productive, and it quickens the achievement of your goals.

- **Meditate**

The brain processes tons of thoughts on any given day. Obviously, not all of these thoughts are positive. So, there's the possibility that your mind holds on to the negative energy generated by those negative thoughts. The purpose of meditation is to clear away those negative energies and maximize your self-awareness capacity. Apart from helping someone get rid of their negative energies, meditation also carries a host of other benefits such as: reducing stress, minimizing anxiety, promoting mental health, increasing your attention span, fight age-induced memory loss, increase an individual's capacity to be kind, and fight away addictions.

STRATEGIES FOR INCREASING SELF-CONTROL

SELF-CONTROL IS SIMPLY AN INDIVIDUAL'S CAPABILITY TO resist temptations and regulate both their thoughts and behaviors. When it comes to overcoming temptations and staying true to who we are, most of us are terrible. Self-control is an important aspect of emotional intelligence that we must cultivate before we attain success.

Benefits of self-control:

1. Improved decision making: our lives are merely sums of our decisions. Whether we succeed or fail, either way, we came to that by decisions. When you have a high level of self-control, you are in a position to make quality decisions because you are uninhibited.

2. Increased chances of success: thanks to self-control, you can make powerful decisions that will help you achieve your goals. Having a skill or talent is no guarantee for success. But you have to make decisions that allow you to thrive.

3. Improve your habits: all habits start with experimenting. Before

someone becomes a drug user, they start out with small doses and gradually get bogged down. But a person with a high level of self-control knows better than to give in to the first temptation. Their zero-tolerance policy against unbecoming habits allows them to become well-rounded individuals.

4. Promotes focus: having self-control means that you are disciplined. You don't just move with the wind. Thus, self-control helps an individual understand what takes precedence in their lives and improves their focus.

Ways of developing self-control:

- **Take a cold shower every morning**

There are a number of health and physiological benefits to taking cold showers each morning, but what's rarely mentioned is the fact that cold showers have a powerful psychological benefit too. Taking cold showers requires that you develop a tough mindset. The hardest part about taking a cold shower is the initial step, i.e., standing beneath the shower, but then once you have done it enough times, it will stop being a challenge, and you will be well on your way towards conquering your fears and developing a tough mindset. Self-control is not something you can achieve overnight. Before you acquire solid discipline, you have to go through numerous experiences that first seem uncomfortable.

- **Eat a balanced diet**

Your emotional health and mental health is at the heart of developing a high level of self-control. Thus, improving an individual's mental health has a positive impact on their effort to master self-control. One of the scientific ways of improving mental health is through diet. Studies show there's a link between the quality of food that a person consumes and their mental health. A balanced diet promotes mental health. In that sense, it helps one get closer to their goal of achieving self-control. A balanced diet generally consists of varied foods, including fruits and vegetables. If you cannot get sufficient vitamins from foods, you may consider eating supplements.

- **Get quality sleep**

Quality sleep doesn't necessarily mean staying in bed for a long period of time. What constitutes quality sleep is mostly the comfort of your bed plus the right environment. By getting quality sleep, you get to reserve the energy of following through on your commitments. One of the reasons why people are unable to stick to their plans is simply because they lack the energy, which is usually a result of, among other things, low-quality sleep. You may want to go to bed early and get out of bed early enough. Quality sleep refreshes you, and you are bound to have the staying power necessary for self-control. Depriving yourself of sleep under the assumption that you'll get more done is a way of ruining progress.

- **Practice**

There are no secrets about attaining self-control. You must stay at work. The harder you work, the more rewards you gain. Most people have a problem with working hard to improve their lives. They seem to think that intense periodical work can supplement consistency, which is nothing but self-deception. But then practicing alone is not enough. You have to find out the tested and proven ways that birth results. Once you figure out how to exert coordinated effort toward the achievement of a goal, then you'll acquire the discipline necessary to stick through the various stages before success.

- **Create long term goals**

The thing about self-control is that it is normally centered on habits. You have to develop habits that emphasize your capacity to be disciplined. And more often than not, you can create these habits in the context of long term goals as opposed to short term goals. Of course, there's nothing wrong with having short term goals, except that they wouldn't hang on for long enough to ensure a new positive habit has taken root within you. Apart from the aspect of creating self-control, long-term goals are also beneficial in terms of creating lasting success and a legacy. One of the areas around which you must learn to create long-term plans is your finances; develop a consistent saving or investing culture since from your youth and you will retire comfortably.

- **Create a schedule**

Unless you craft a timetable, you are not likely to make productive use of your time. Most often, when we are engaged in emotionally-rewarding activities, we stop paying attention to the lapse of time. And this puts us in a situation whereby we are afraid of giving up this emotionally pleasant activity. But when you have a schedule, you have unity in your goals. Having a schedule not only saves you time but also hastens the realization of your dreams.

- **Embrace change**

We are living in the age of information, and you can be sure that companies that have been around for quite a while had to adopt, and those who resisted change are now long buried. Change doesn't necessarily mean you have entered "nasty" territory. And even if it's nasty, there are other people fighting it out too. Before you are an emotionally intelligent person, you will have to endure an uncomfortable phase. Such experiences might break those who have brittle hearts, but then again, such experiences are necessary for growth.

- **Journaling**

For journaling to be an effective method, you have to perform it on the regular, as opposed to putting in one entry until days or weeks later. The purpose of journaling is to record the various thoughts swirling in your head at various times of the day. Also, journaling helps capture the various experiences you encounter in a normal day. Apart from taking down the details and thus promoting accuracy when it comes to relating various experiences, journaling also carries a powerful cathartic effect. No one is ever immune to terrible thoughts. But then journaling can help you to fight away negativity. Journaling helps an individual gain a deep understanding of what they truly are. It brings out an individual's habits and tendencies to the fore. This helps people realize what they are truly like.

- **Reading**

Acquiring emotional intelligence is not about just giving stuff away, but it's also about taking something in. In the world we live in, knowledge is a tremendous tool. You have to have quality thoughts in order to make progress. One of the best ways of acquiring knowledge is through reading books. But then instead of sticking to books that sharpen your expertise only, you might want to widen your focus. Reading will help you absorb important knowledge that will go towards creating a better life for you. Apart from boosting both your intelligence and emotional quotient, reading is also fun. Depending on the personality of the writer, you may have quite a nice time reading through their works.

- **Socialize**

Another awesome way of improving your emotional intelligence is through meeting other people. This is a very important exercise because it strengthens your social skills. At the end of the day, your social skills are far more important than even your technical skills. Human beings are the gatekeepers of whatever you want, and so you must know how to deal with them. If you are naturally reserved, don't make it an excuse, for you can be an introvert band yet have sharp communication and social skills. When you become savvy at connecting with different human beings, you gain so much power.

- **Exercising**

The biggest deterrent to emotional wellbeing is stress. If you are stressed out, you are hardly going to have thought clarity, and ultimately, you are going to make poor decisions. But then exercising is one of the best ways of getting rid of stress. Develop a habit of training your body, whether lightly or heavily, and it will improve both your mental and emotional health.

- **Embrace emotional distress**

At the end of the day, discipline is about sticking to your principles even when it makes you uncomfortable. So, learn to embrace emotional discomfort. If you are not tolerant to pain, it means that you will easily give up. Emotional intelligence is about developing staying power. You have to become emotionally tough and resist instant gratification because they usually amount to traps.

STRATEGIES FOR INCREASING MOTIVATION

Self-motivation is another sign of emotional intelligence. When we say that someone is self-motivated, we mean that they have a deep reason that compels them to work towards the achievement of their goals. Being motivated is critical because it gives on the staying power. Normally, before you achieve success, it won't be a smooth run. If you lack self-motivation, you won't be able to hang on until things get better. But if you are self-motivated, you will still show up until there's a breakthrough. For instance, there are a number of Hollywood stars who encountered seemingly insurmountable challenges at the start of their careers, but because they were self-motivated, they hang on until they had a breakthrough.

It doesn't matter what you are working towards, but you have to be self-motivated so that most importantly you may have the staying power

Advantages of being self-motivated:

1. It helps you develop your vision: all the work you are doing on a daily basis is calculated to have a particular impact within a certain time frame. Your vision is simply the transformation that you want to affect whether it's in your life or in other people's lives. Being self-motivated helps you stay clear about what you want to achieve.

2. It helps you overcome indecisiveness: when you are motivated, you are also in a position to come up with creative ways of making decisions. And this ensures that you are not bogged down by indecisiveness.

3. It helps you overcome negative energy: there's an overabundance of negative energy in the world. If you are not careful, negativity could easily take over and stop you from achieving your dreams. But being motivated permits you to stay focused upon what truly matters.

4. It allows you to express your highest capabilities: self-motivation is what pushes an individual to bring out the X factor – their best performance. It is not necessarily so as to win people's praise but as a way to challenge oneself and to see how deep their potential extends.

Strategies for boosting motivation:

- **Just get started**

If you just sit on a couch and just think about what needs to be done, you will hardly ever get started. But then if you take the first bold step of action, you'll be well on your way toward becoming a motivated person. You may have great ideas on paper, but if there's no action to back it up, the ideas on their own won't have any meaning.

- **Start small**

One of the reasons why people start procrastinating is simply because they put impossibly high standards for themselves. And this keeps them from taking the initial step. So, begin by setting achievable goals, and you will have no fear of taking action. It doesn't matter how you begin, but as long as there's potential in your idea, there's a limitless room for expansion.

- **Get rid of distractions**

Distractions are some of the things that keep you from fulfilling your goals. They take your attention away from what needs to be done. Some of the commonest forms of distraction include our mobile phones and TVs. When you are about to undertake a major activity, ensure that you put away potential sources of distractions, and focus your attention on the task at hand.

- **Become accountable**

The easiest way to check yourself is to start caring about how you spend your resources like time and money. For most of us, it can be quite hard to keep ourselves in line, but then we are supposed to ask other people to hold us accountable. Some of the best candidates for this task include our friends and relatives. For instance, we can have our friends monitor our spending habits and usage of time.

- **Delegate tasks**

It is important to delegate tasks that can be effectively handled by other people without loss of quality or bogging down the process. The importance of delegating tasks is that you get to make your work easier which encourages you to get started and it also puts you in a team spirit as you now know that there's a team relying on your diligence. This helps you bring forth your hard-working spirit.

- **Watch inspiring media**

When people speak of the effects of technology, it is mostly on a negative tone, highlighting the quick access to negative media like porn, which has a terrible impact on people's work ethic. But, then, the same technology makes for easier access to positive media. You can look for blogs, podcasts, and movies that radiate positivity. You can look at videos along your line of work. Such content should enable you to create a great life for yourself.

- **The power of music**

Studies have shown that music bears a lot of power. Whenever you find yourself needing to exert a lot of mental resources on a task, just put on some music in the background, and this is going to improve your cognitive functions. The right kind of music will boost your brain power and help you achieve your important life goals.

- **Be optimistic**

In the face of challenges, it is so easy to develop a pessimistic attitude. But then such an attitude would keep you from being proactive. It takes effort to be an optimistic person, but the rewards are worth it. Being optimistic is about developing sufficient positive mental energy that keeps you taking the right steps in life. Optimism allows you to make the best decisions that will fast track you to success.

- **Stop being harsh on yourself**

Some people are unable to stay motivated simply because they are too hard on themselves. There's nothing alien about failure. It happens to each one of us. But then what matters is how you follow on your failure. Instead of putting your hands up and crying defeat, you should get back to work with a renewed determination. The easiest way to be accepting of failure is always to give yourself a second chance.

- **Learn from your mistakes**

Instead of letting your mistakes bog you down, you might want actually to get inspired by them. Look at your mistakes objectively and understand where you have gone wrong. This should help you understand what you must do and what you must not do in order to arrive at your goal.

- **Stop comparing yourself to the world**

When you compare yourself to the world, you not only risk losing motivation but your self-worth as well. In this age of social media, it is so easy to try to measure where you stand in the world and realize that your achievements are pretty insignificant. Of course, this makes you feel bad. But you have no reason to feel bad about your achievements! For you never know the kind of head start that everybody else was lucky to have. When you stop comparing yourself to the world, you will start appreciating what you have.

- **Keep your eyes at the end goal**

Any moment you feel un-motivated, just remind yourself why you are doing this. Always keep your eyes on the prize. For instance, if you are building a business, and you feel as though it is taking too much of your resources and there are no returns, instead of giving up, just think about how badly you want to free yourself from your daytime job. Such a thought should help you keep grinding the midnight oil as you wait for a breakthrough.

- **Have gratitude**

Unless you are grateful for what you have, you will hardly make progress in life. Having gratitude means that you appreciate what you already have. It can make the biggest difference between happiness and desolation. Grateful people don't hold material things as more important than virtues. But ungrateful people place material possessions above all else. Such a mentality causes them to irritate their allies, and the results are ugly.

- **Take breaks**

You don't have a bottomless pit of motivation within you. It's more like a banking situation. You have to make constant deposits in order to be able to withdraw. This is what taking a break is about. Get away from all the mind-numbing activities and "recharge" so that when you get back, you will have sufficient energy to tackle your challenges.

- **Physical training**

Performing physical exercises is a vital endeavor. Physical training comes with a host of health benefits including; strengthened immune system, improved digestion, heart health, and brain health. Exercising also promotes good looks, which makes a person feel good about themselves. Additionally, exercising improves an individual's emotional health and makes them feel good about themselves.

- **Reward yourself**

You can improve your motivation by always rewarding yourself for the milestones you complete. The more goals you achieve, the more you convince your subconscious mind that you are indeed worthy of success. For that reason, it is critical to set goals that you can actually achieve. And rewarding yourself is not necessarily about splashing millions. Doing something that gives you a rush of adrenaline, e.g., skydiving – may very well be enough reward for some people.

WAYS TO IMPROVE EMPATHY

Empathy is what makes you stop along the aisle of a supermarket to help a senior citizen get the exact product that he wants. Well-adjusted people have empathy for others. But people with dark personalities like narcissism and psychopathy lack in empathy.

Empathy is an individual's capability to sense other people's feelings and figure out what it must be like. Such realization helps an individual act in an appropriate manner. Admittedly, there's not enough empathy to go round. And many of us are vicious with one another.

Empathy indicates that an individual has high emotional intelligence. But what are some of the things we can do in order to boost empathy?

- **Give people a chance to speak**

Perhaps you are a talkative person who struggles with letting other people contribute to the conversation. Thus, it can be a bit hard to realize what's going on in your friend's world. You have to learn to become interested in what people are doing, and it will help you understand their lives. At the end of the day, we are all hurting humans, and we need to support each other in order to move up collectively.

- **Travel more**

The hard economic times don't allow us to keep moving at our wish. And then there's also the fact that some people have a strong nesting instinct, which discourages them from going from one place to another. Once they find their ideal location, then they want to settle for forever in that area. Unless you have traveled extensively, you are less likely to have empathy for other people.

- **Learn a new skill**

Never overestimate people's capacity to be self-sufficient. If someone is in the service industry, they will become less and less effective as the years fade away, and then, it will get to a point when the formerly glorious star now becomes a liability and, even worse, fail to function. The more we expand our skill set, the more we realize people who are in need of us. Thus, such activities should not make us feel special or above everyone else, but rather they should make us feel humbled.

- **Develop your conversation skills**

Unless you have sharp conversation skills, you are unlikely to have objective communication. But when you have stellar conversation skills, you are in a position to articulate various situations and develop clear concepts. Before you can have empathy for someone, you first need to understand where they are coming from. But then it will take sharp communication skills to ensure that you have an articulate conversation.

- **Improve your reading culture**

Books serve the purpose of ridding us of ignorance. No one knows it all. It doesn't matter where you are in life, but you will always stand to gain from reading new books. It will also open you up to new ways of being an empathetic person. For instance, you may get to learn of vulnerable people or situations that require consideration.

- **Solicit feedback**

In as much as we might think that we have figured out what we are like, the truth is that other people have a more authentic understanding of what we are really like because they have watched us for a long time. If you'd like an honest opinion about your behaviors and tendencies, you may want to ask your trusted friend to reveal both your positive and negative side. Ensure that you create strong bonds with various people who can comfortably talk about both your weaknesses and strengths. Once you have acquired that feedback, it becomes easier – moving forward – to treat people in a much more empathetic manner.

- **Notice your biases**

Various scientific studies have shown us many times over that each one of us holds some form of bias. It can be either conscious or unconscious bias. But either way, it denies you the chance to treat that person in an honest manner. In some contexts, seemingly empathetic actions may amount to what needed to be done anyway. For instance, in dangerous residences where different people get profiled, mere actions of helping the vulnerable seem such a big deal when it's the right thing anyway.

- **Stop interrupting others**

If you have a tendency of interrupting others as they speak, they might end up resenting you and clamming up. People can be extremely varied in how they relate to one another. When you meet new people, learn to give yourself ample time to allow them to express themselves in their own words. This allows them to bring out precisely their circumstances.

- **Smile**

Smiling has long been recognized as the standard positive body language across the world. It doesn't matter that you don't speak the same language as someone else. When you have a habit of smiling, people start being welcoming toward you, and now, the challenge is finding a way to communicate and preserve such moments in the pages of time. Scientific research also shows that smiling causes the body to secrete feel-good hormones, like dopamine. This causes the double effect of making you happy as well as being kind to another person.

- **Give people their due credit**

Nothing makes a person feel more appreciated than being acknowledged openly. Thus, if someone collaborated with you or if you sought assistance on a matter, it is wise to state their role in the matter, especially if whatever you sought help on became successful. Acknowledging the positive input of people is a great thing. On the other hand, stifling people and failing to give them their due credit not only saddens them but may very well break their resolve.

- **Ask people for their opinions**

The ego is an incredibly powerful beast. It wants to put you in a dominant position. But such behavior doesn't aid your capacity to be empathetic. Instead, it promotes your narcissistic tendencies. Thus, you must learn to ask people about their opinions. Such behavior encourages people to drop their guard and open up to you. Once someone is comfortable around you, they may proceed to reveal their secrets, and you have a chance to show them empathy. But, then, simply because you want to show empathy is no invitation to be particularly nosy. Stay aware of their micro-expressions and respect their right to privacy.

- **Master nonverbal cues**

Most messages are passed through actions, expressions, and tonal variations than through actual words. Research shows that communication is about 90% nonverbal and only 10% verbal. This means in order to get what the other person is saying you have to be aware of their nonverbal cues. So, improve your capacity of detecting changes in facial expressions, tonal variety, and other forms of body language. This will help you understand other people much more clearly. And the more you become skilled at mastering nonverbal cues, the more endearing you become to other people.

- **Avoid multitasking while talking to others**

For one, when you indulge in some other activities while you talk to another person, it shows that you don't give them respect. It can cause the other person to have a terrible conception of you. And then you wouldn't have a connection with that person. Ensure that you give the other person your undivided attention. This goes a long way in making you trustworthy. And it increases the likelihood of the other person opening up and being vulnerable.

- **Be open and vulnerable**

Empathy is often applicable to a situation where people are honest. For instance, if you make yourself appear to be some sort of superhuman, people will raise their eyebrows and take an instant dislike to you. People are full faults. And they gravitate towards other people who seem to have faults. When you are open and vulnerable, you make yourself appear to have faults, and this draws in other people, and in that context, you have a chance of deepening your empathy.

- **Be more flexible**

Instead of having a rigid mindset, you want to be a bit more flexible. Being flexible encourages your empathetic side as well as your creative side. It is also an indication that you don't have major personality disorders like narcissism or psychopathy. People who have dark personalities are less likely to renege on their demands even if they are shown how unreasonable they are. Being flexible allows you to form great partnerships with other people and make progress in life.

- **Have patience and be supportive**

If you are an overbearing person, you are likely to turn off people and your capacity to show empathy will be limited. You have to be patient with others. It shows that you genuinely care about them, and you want them to make progress in life. Apart from having patience, you have also to encourage people. Give them guidance into the proper way of doing things and support your reasoning in a logical way. By being patient with people, you allow them to exploit their full potential.

WAYS TO DEVELOP SOCIAL SKILLS

Human beings are social animals. We need to interact with each other in order to fulfill our important psychological and physical needs. It doesn't matter what our work entails, but we will always rely on each other. So, when we talk of social skills, we are talking about our capacity to interact with other human beings through both verbal and nonverbal means. People who have high emotional intelligence are pretty good at interacting with others in social settings. And for that reason, they stand a far better chance of fulfilling their needs than people who are lacking in social skills. But the great thing is that social skills are not ingrained in the DNA. They are merely skills, and anyone with a will can master them. The following are some ways of developing your social skills:

- **Show interest in other people**

The problem with most people who are lacking in social skills is that they expect the world to surrender at their feet. It doesn't work that way. You should be proactive and take an interest in other people's lives as opposed to waiting for them to take an interest in you. So, start approaching people and asking about their lives; it will help you form a positive relationship with them.

- **Improve your body language**

Don't be so focused on what you are going to tell people that you forget to work on how you are going to say it. After all, nonverbal communication is what really matters. Your body language is much more important than your words. If you are giving a speech, ensure that you seem enthusiastic, so that you may draw people in.

- **Speak clearly**

Nothing is worse than having a mumbled speaking voice. It stops people from getting your message. In order to have a clear voice, there are no two ways about it: you have to put in the effort and practice. So, see to it that you work on your voice on a daily basis, and you'll soon be in a position to speak with clarity.

- **Have the right tone**

Apart from the fact that message delivery is impacted by your tone, it is also a gauge of your level of confidence. You don't want to sound too loud or too soft. You have to come up with the right tone that will make everyone comfortable. Just as it is necessary to practice in order to improve your speaking clarity, you can practice improving your tone as well, but then understand there are limits.

You won't always have the tone that you want to if your genetics don't allow it.

- **Start to listen to others actively**

Most people want to talk about themselves, and they forget that in order to carry the conversation forward, they need to also listen to what the other person is saying. Active listening is about paying full attention to the other person. It involves facing them fully, establishing eye contact, and mirroring back their actions, among other things. When you are an active listener, people will take a liking to you.

- **Get out of your comfort zone**

Of course, socializing at your local church is much easier because you have been part of that church for decades and you have cordial relations with most members. How about you take on a challenge? Travel far away in new states and attend conferences and still try to socialize with people. In a new setting, you are likely to be self-conscious, but as long as you are aware of the basics, you should do just fine.

- **Avoid multitasking during conversations**

If you are suddenly struck by an urge to do something while in the middle of a conversation, it would be more courteous to ask the other person of permission, as opposed to going right into it. For instance, you might have the urge to make a phone call or send a text message, so you just ask the person to give you a second to make that phone call or send that text message.

- **Just be assertive**

This means you should not be overbearing and at the same time, you shouldn't let people through at your expense. An assertive person expresses their needs or opinions in a truthful manner, and they are careful not to violate other people's rights. Sadly, most of us are either aggressive or passive-aggressive, both of which are undesirable traits that indicate arrogance and manipulation, respectively, and they turn people away from us. Some people are scared of being assertive, thinking that it will make people have a less than honorable opinion of them, but on the contrary, being assertive will win you more allies and, in turn, more respect.

- **Master the art of timing**

Nothing would put a strain between two people than an argument that comes up in an inopportune moment. For that reason, you have to be incredibly mindful of when you bring up certain discussions. For instance, if someone owes you money, would it be fair to wait until they are surrounded by friends and family, and then go ahead to ask for your money back? Of course, it is not a crime that you are asking your money back, but the fact that they are surrounded by friends and family means that you have embarrassed them, and your friendship will barely survive that.

- **Choose the right communication channel**

In as much as you like word of mouth over any other method of communication, sometimes you may have to choose a different medium in order to convey the message precisely. For instance, if you are coming up with a complex thought that you need to share with your friends or acquaintances, it would be more effective sending them a detailed email as opposed to speaking to them on the phone. So, always ensure that you match your message with the right communication tool.

- **Be open minded**

We live in a world of billions of people. It is unlikely that most of us have had similar experiences. And this means that our perceptions and our beliefs are not necessarily similar. Thus, we have to be accommodating of people who hold different opinions than us. This is not to mean that we are inferior or superior to them, but rather, we are civil even in our disagreements. It's totally okay to agree to disagree and focus on what you both agree on. But never have the attitude that "my way is the only way."

- **Create a positive mindset**

Instead of always having a pessimistic view of life, try to cultivate a positive mindset. People are drawn towards people who seem to be enjoying life, and this comes from having a positive mentality. On the other hand, being negative only serves to wreak havoc, and turn people away from you. One of the best ways to create a positive mindset is by ensuring that you are surrounded by positive individuals. This is because you eventually become like your close friends.

- **Accept constructive criticism**

Not every criticism is made in bad faith. Some people criticize you hoping that you will take corrective measures. This is called constructive criticism. As a human being, you are not designed to be perfect. So, being criticized is perfectly normal. Always study the source of criticism to understand whether they are motivated by ill or good intentions. Rejecting constructive criticism is an indication of pride or a dark personality, and it would hold you back from developing your social skills.

- **Respect people**

At the end of the day, you are looking for respect, but then you have to give others respect in order to be respected back. It starts with the seemingly small affairs like the proper attitude, word selection, saying thank you, and keeping good manners. It is through respecting people that you get to build a good reputation. And in these streets, reputation is everything.

- **Don't try to change what you are**

People can spot fake from a mile off. Trying to hide the person that you are can only have a bitter ending. Oscar Wilde famously said that everyone ought to be themselves because everyone else is already taken. Of course, this is no invitation to upset people just because you are yourself. You just shouldn't alter yourself in order to fit people's expectations of you.

- **Empathize with people**

Instead of being the person that laughs out loud when you hear that your friends are in trouble, you should be the person that lends a helping hand. Having empathy goes a long way in tightening friendships as it involves sacrifice. Life is full of challenges. And the reason why it's important to show others empathy is that when you face challenges yourself – a sure thing – you will have someone to depend on.

- **Increase your confidence**

You cannot make any progress in your social life without having confidence. And confidence is not like a pill that you swallow. It is a skill that must be continually developed. When you are fully confident of yourself and your abilities, you are in a position to enjoy a fulfilling social life.

HOW EMOTIONAL INTELLIGENCE IMPROVES YOUR LIFE

Every person has a goal or a cluster of goals that they are looking forward to achieving. But is there any tested and proven formula for achieving success? Well, there might not be a sure formula, but emotional intelligence is a vital ingredient for success. These are some of the impacts of emotional intelligence in a person's life that help them become a success story:

- **It helps you get rid of fear**

In most cases, the one monster standing between you and your goals is fear. But then fear is rooted in ignorance. If you fail to understand what is happening, you are likely to become overwhelmed by fear. But then emotional intelligence helps you understand how your mind processes emotions, and how various emotions drive the habits of other people, and such knowledge empowers you to act without fear.

- **It promotes your social skills**

When we talk of success, it is hard to remove the factor of people. This is because it takes people to make things happen. But then you have to have social skills in order to form great relationships with people. For this reason, an averagely gifted person with above-average social skills stands a far better chance of succeeding than a supremely talented person with mediocre social skills. People tend to do business with those that they like. Thus, you have to develop your social skills so that you can form great relationships with others.

- **It makes you more decisive**

We live in a fast-moving world. If you are not just as fast, you are left behind. You have to make big decisions within a short frame of time. And most people have a problem making great decisions within such a limited time. But then emotional intelligence grants them the ability to process various factors pretty fast and come up with a great decision.

- **More accepting of change**

Change is the only constant. As long as humans live on this earth, things will be changing, sometimes slowly and sometimes pretty fast. Low emotional intelligence is linked with resisting change, but a high emotional intelligence helps you adapt to change very quickly. This makes you have an edge.

- **It improves your capacity to listen**

People with low emotional intelligence don't actually listen to the way it's supposed to be done. This is because they don't process various aspects of the conversation that pass across an important message. But when you have a high level of emotional intelligence, you are in a position to understand the nuances, and the various nonverbal cues, that add to the spoken message. Being a good listener is one of the main things that make a person endearing. And being a good listener reduces chances of miscommunication and also minimizes chances of making errors. Also being a good listener improves your capacity to make sound and accurate decisions.

- **You become open minded**

Let's assume that you were born in a very religious family. You are likely to have grown up holding strong Christian beliefs. For instance, homosexuality may have been taboo, and that people who engaged in homosexual intercourse you believed they'd fan the embers of hell after their time on this earth, right? Except, on the other hand, research shows that homosexuality is perfectly natural. Of course, there's going to be a difference of opinion once you encounter a gay. You may have your differences, but then, you may still decide to treat them with respect because at the end of the day, what matters is that they are every bit as human as you. If the evidence is overwhelming that homosexuality is indeed a thing from nature, you might abandon your old belief and become accepting of homosexual relations. That'd be a major sign of high emotional intelligence. But for someone with low emotional intelligence, they can't ever think of abandoning their stances even when confronted by overwhelming proof to the contrary.

- **It toughens you up**

In most cases, it takes a vicious psychological fight to acquire anything worth having. This is because resources are limited, and people yearning for those resources are much too many. So, you have to have the emotional makeup of a winner in order to surmount these obstacles and achieve your goals. Emotional intelligence helps you have the staying power even when things aren't going as per plan. And this ability to hang on until circumstances are tight usually makes all the difference. People with low emotional intelligence are likely to have a fixed mindset about how success must come to them, and if it doesn't go as they expected, as is usually the case, they quickly give up and find someone or something to blame. But, then, high emotional intelligence toughens up your spirit, and you are ready to ride the whole journey.

- **It allows you to focus on your priorities**

Success means various things for different people. For instance, if you came from a broken family, and you are really hurting, maybe your idea of success is not merely creating a profitable business but ensuring that you bring up a loving family. So, if family is your priority, it means that you may have to pass on deals that come between you and your family. Of course, you care about making money, but not as much as keeping your loved ones happy. People who scale the heights of success are good at guarding their priorities. When you acquire a high level of emotional intelligence, you will be in a position to determine your priorities and guard them. This improves your emotional health and gives you the energy to pursue your best life.

- **It helps you weigh the good and bad qualities in others**

No one is an angel. We are all faulty in one way or another. But our pride might keep us from seeing our faults. But that is beside the point. In order to achieve success, you must include other people in your plans. But these people come with both strengths and weakness, both the good and the bad. If you can somehow figure out their strengths and weaknesses, then you can match them with activities that allow them to capitalize on their strengths. This gives everyone a decent chance of success. And it makes the world a much better place.

- **It increases your motivation**

Motivation is the force behind every success. You have to have a reason as to why you want a particular outcome. And this reason is what compels you to become a fighter and achieve your goal. People with high emotional intelligence are bound to have clarity of thought about why they want to achieve a specific thing. And also they are bound to be relentless in their efforts to achieve their goal. In the journey to your goal, you won't always be in the mood to put in the work, but then you must motivate yourself to work hard anyway, even if results are not forthcoming, knowing too well that better days are ahead.

- **It gives you an optimistic mindset**

Happiness is not merely about the acquisition of material things. It is also about your emotional health. There are far many wealthy people who lead chaotic lives. And at the same time, there are many people of average income who lead what can be termed as a "happy life." Optimism is the cornerstone of happiness as we know it. People with high emotional intelligence tend to be particularly optimistic. And such mindset informs their decisions, and in the long run, it pays off. On the other hand, pessimists believe that the world is conspiring against them, which causes them to lose hope and take poor decisions that ultimately destabilize them.

- **It allows you to set healthy boundaries**

Time is a limited resource, and if you are functioning in any position of power, most people must be looking to take your time. But then you must be careful how you spend your time lest you ruin yourself along with what you have built. This is the purpose of setting boundaries. Some people might say that you have too high an opinion of yourself for setting boundaries but take it for what it is: negative criticism. Healthy boundaries allow you to safeguard your sanity and have a handle on how you spend your time. Boundaries instill a sense of discipline too. They are critical in the journey to success.

- **The ability to say "No."**

Most people are afraid – or ashamed – of saying "No." It's simply because they don't want to upset other people and risk being cast out of their social circles. Such habits result in people making self-inhibiting decisions that hinder them from achieving the success that they deserve. But then developing your emotional intelligence opens you up to a new perspective. You realize that it is not wrong to actually put your interests first.

HOW TO PRACTICE GRATITUDE

It's rare to find a person who's actually contented with what they have and not looking to acquire more. It's precisely why the world's richest men haven't yet stopped showing up in their offices. They – like everybody else – want more. But in as much as we want to complete one milestone after another, we must not lose sight of what we already have. Being grateful is simply having an appreciation for what you have already acquired or received. The world is keen to notice people who are grateful. Many wealthy people have confessed that the secret to their riches is their gratitude.

But what are some of the ways that one may practice gratitude?

- **Say "Thank you" a lot more**

Let's say you are in a meeting and you suddenly have to sign a document except that you have no pen. So, you turn around to your colleague, a sweet, vibrant woman, and borrow their pen. So you sign away at the document, toss the pen back, and walk off. What kind of impression would you make of yourself? Would that woman be ecstatic about lending you a helping hand again? Of course not. It's the simple things like saying "Thank you" that truly matter when it comes to building a reputation. Thus, if someone assists you in any way, always say, "Thank you."

- **Give credit**

We see this lot amongst Silicone Valley tycoons. Let's say a multi-millionaire investor has an idea, but it is actually a few young developers that perform the bulk of the work before an idea becomes successful. But once it's out there, the millionaire jumps from one studio to the next as they seek glory, never once mentioning the team behind success. Even though the developers signed nondisclosure agreements, it still stands to reason that the investor acknowledges being assisted. The problem with taking all credit is that it elevates you to god-status, an attitude that repels away people, for people want to see that you get help like everyone else, that you have got faults, you're not a god among mortals.

- **Realize each day is a gift**

If you have achieved a few successes in your life, you can easily develop the god-complex and think that everything must flow according to your wishes. That's a dangerous mindset. Even as you make your plans, you should always recognize the uncertainty of life. There are billions of us on earth, and why should you count yourself someone special? Approach every day as though it were a gift – for it actually is – and make the best of your life so that you are free of guilt.

- **Keep a gratitude journal**

If you are a keen person, you will have many things to be thankful for on a daily basis. But it doesn't help just observing them through your mind's eye. You should instead keep a journal where you enter the various things that you are grateful for. It can be your health, your family, and the little experiences you have with other people as you go about your business.

- **Spend time in nature**

Although modern technology has made life exceedingly easy, it has also imposed various limitations on us. For instance, we hardly create time for outdoor activities anymore. Stepping out of your house and wandering into the woods can be extremely relaxing. So, make it a habit of spending time in nature. Come up with creative ideas that you may explore while you spend time in nature. It will improve your emotional health and bequeath you more vitality.

- **Stop taking people for granted**

If you are a millionaire and you live in an apartment alone with your house help, never look down on them, or treat them badly, for you might not know how valuable they are until you lose them. So, ensure that you always treat people with decorum. Also, understand that there's a force in life known as karma. This is what the oppressed, the browbeaten, and the exploited people rely on to get their vengeance against those who hurt them. It is basically the idea of "If you can dish it, you should also be prepared to receive it." But all this can be avoided by just being a decent person that appreciates the people in his life.

- **Make parties for your birthdays and anniversaries**

Some people are so tight with their money that they hardly spoil themselves on their great day. That's pointless. If you can afford it, there's no reason that you shouldn't celebrate your important days like birthday and wedding anniversary. It is a sign that you still value yourself and are proud of the path that you have taken in life. Making parties is also a great opportunity to bring together your loved ones and friends and create memorable times.

- **Compliment other people**

Whether a compliment is received well or badly depends on how you say it. Avoid complimenting people's body parts and lean towards professional achievements. This shows them that you actually have good intentions. And then again don't compliment someone like a million times in a single day. It reeks of desperation, and the next time they see you from afar, they might run to hide.

- **Realize that you are enough**

Life is full of heartache, and in most cases, this pain comes from other people, or rather the deeds and misdeeds of other people. Love can breed pain. Lack of love can breed even worse pain. So, there's pain either way. But instead of drowning in misery understand that you are all you need. Once you straighten your mindset and recognize that you are enough, then you'll be well on your way toward living your best life possible. So many young people waste their lives away as a result of nasty love affairs, and it can set them up for dysfunctional adult life.

- **Put your family first**

When you hear it being said that no one cares about you except your family, know that there's some truth to that statement. But this is not to mean that the world is your enemy. That's just how life is. It's everyone for himself. But it helps to have a family that you know you can depend on. It takes time and effort to create tight family relations and be proud of one another. Your family can be the biggest source of joy, but in the same breath, it can be the biggest source of disappointment, so that you are caught in a web of tremendous animosity.

- **Stop complaining**

One of the mysteries of life is that those who have all the reasons to complain hardly ever do so, but those who have no reason to complain are actually the loudest complainers. What do I mean? You live in a first world country, and you have surplus access to all your basic needs, and you can even afford some luxuries. But you keep complaining about how everything is going to the dogs. Have you ever thought about the human beings across the world who face hunger and starvation; and get raped and killed by ruthless militia? The point is, grow some balls, and fight for success with a patient attitude. The funny thing is that if the government provides an instant solution to your problem, you'll still find something else to complain about.

- **Don't lose your cool during tough times**

If you want to see the true character of a man just watch them in their time of adversity. Most of us are wont to lose it. We would blame everything else but us for the hardship we are going through. But then this takes away our capacity to be grateful. On the other hand, if we can meet hardship and persecution with calm patience, it is a sign that we appreciate our struggle. And as long as we live, there'll always be challenges in our lives, but we must develop better ways of addressing them.

- **Quit regretting**

There are some decisions we took in the past that come back to haunt us. Whenever you find yourself in such a situation, you must resist. Keep your eyes to the fore. The present moment and the future is all that matters. But you cannot prepare for your future if you are stuck in the past. Regrets will only ruin your mental composure and cause you untold pain. If you hurt someone back then or if someone hurt you, try to go the reconciliatory route, but then make sure you don't relive the nasty emotional bomb that you suffered back then.

- **Take care of yourself**

Since you are still alive, you have every reason to thank yourself. People and the state have helped you along your journey, yes, but it was you that did most of the work. You believed in yourself and took action. So, the best reward you can give yourself is simply to take care of yourself. Eat a balanced diet, exercise, get enough quality sleep, socialize, etc.

TECHNIQUES FOR DEVELOPING PATIENCE

Think of any successful person that you know of, both internationally and domestically. What do they have in common? They are patient. Their success is a result of many years of hard work. Apart from enduring challenges they still had to wait for various processes to be finished and results to come back, they had to board planes, talk to executives, and perform a number of exercises all in a bid to attain their goal. Eventually, their patience paid off.

Unless you have superhuman powers, it's not possible to set a long term goal today and make it a reality tomorrow. They are called long term for a reason. If you are still interested in making your dream come true, you have to take the long, hard route of exercising some patience.

- **Have a growth mentality**

Being patient is all about believing that good times are ahead.

Thus, you have to have the right mindset so that you can be in a position to make progress in life. Most people have trouble making progress in life simply because they never encourage themselves to make positive decisions in life.

- **Write down your goal**

One of the problems that people have is having abstracting goals. And abstract goals deny you the chance to be proactive in your life. If you want to increase your fighting spirit, you have to write down your goals, and then internalize them into your psyche. This will help you become much of a fighter. When writing down your goal, ensure that it adheres to the following standards:

1. Specific: your goal must be as specific as possible. For instance, it is not enough to say, "I want to be rich by the end of this year." But rather you should say, "I want to make $10M by the end of 2019."

2. Measurable: your goal should be measurable too. You have to be able to establish how your goal has progressed. If you cannot measure the progress of your goal, then you would hardly determine what needs to be done.

3. Attainable: this is the most important quality. Your goals should be within your reach. If you create goals that you obviously won't come true, you only set yourself up for disappointment plus you risk inviting antagonism from your subconscious mind.

- **Have more than one approaches**

Accomplishing your goals is not a walk in the park. You need to have a great fighting spirit that doesn't let you give up easily. Additionally, you need to have more than one strategies of accomplishing what you want. Tap into your creative side and see what needs to be done every time you hit the wall. Most people give up because they fail to come up with different ways of facing the same challenge.

- **Break your goals down**

Who says that your goal needs to be one big, seemingly insurmountable challenge? It's totally okay to break your goal down into sub-goals. This will make the whole process much more interesting. When you break down your goal, you stand a better chance of achieving these goals, and it will help you make quick progress. On the other hand, having long term goals that are barely simplified can exert a lot of pressure on you.

- **Realize the stuff that you cannot control**

Having patience is, for the most part, a mental thing. If you are mentally weak, you will lose your courage, and give in to the pressure. One of the ways you can ensure that you remain mentally tough is by realizing the stuff that you cannot control. There might be factors outside of your control that will influence the results that you anticipate. For instance, if you have made an application, whether the results come back positive or negative is out of your control; it is upon the governing authorities to decide. But then a lot of people are held hostage by obsessing over matters that they have no control over, and this denies them the ability to be strong.

- **Know what triggers your emotions**

A big part of staying true to your goals is emotional stability. You have to guard yourself against emotional weaknesses because it is during such times that you are likely to lose your patience. In order to be emotionally strong, you have to have an awareness of the things that trigger your emotions. For instance, if you are prone to get angry every time you encounter someone that tried to hurt you, understand that that person is an emotional trigger, and do your best to stay away from them. Being emotionally weak can cause you to not only lose your patience but also make poor decisions.

- **Enjoy the process**

Who says that being patient has to be a long and tedious process that lacks in fun? It doesn't matter your line of work, but you can always come up with fun activities as you wait for your breakthrough. For instance, if you are working on your business, running into losses month after month, it's very easy to become overwhelmed by the losses and perceive life as torturous. Such an attitude would likely send you into depression. The alternative is to play down your negative thoughts. And this can be achieved through creative fun. For instance, you may come up with games to play in your free time. When you manage to play down your negative thoughts, you are in a better position to increase your positive mental energy and achieve your dreams.

- **Utilize relaxation techniques**

When you are running out of patience, you are at risk of becoming mentally unstable. And in such a situation, you are prone to make poor decisions. The best way to ensure that you don't make poor decisions is by indulging in various relaxation techniques such as deep breathing and meditating. Deep breathing involves sitting in a most comfortable place and taking air in and out, slowly. This restores calm to your mind and helps you improve the quality of your life.

- **Become aware of the range of your emotions**

Each person has a set of emotions that they are likely to experience in various situations of their lives. Thus it would be wise to master the emotions that you are likely to experience. This allows you to come up with counteractive measures. Emotional instability is the number one reason people give up easily. But when you are aware of the nature of your emotions, it becomes easier to create remedies.

- **Take a break**

Simply because you took a break doesn't mean that you gave up on your dreams. Understand that making your dreams come true can sometimes be a grueling task. If you take a break, you get to revitalize yourself and come back with a renewed zeal. Most people tend to work themselves into exhaustion until they have no choice but to give up. But then you have to have a great understanding of self so that you might able to realize when you are running out of energy and take a rest.

- **Have gratitude**

The most ambitious people of the world seem to agree on one thing: gratitude is critical for success. You have to look around you and appreciate what you already have. And for the most part, you have a lot to be thankful for your family, your career, friends, and health. When you have a spirit of gratitude, it instills in you a sense of discipline. You realize what truly matters in life. And you keep applying yourself toward the achievement of your goals.

- **Improve your lifestyle**

Your lifestyle has a great impact on your emotional stability. Being patient is about having prime mental health. So, ensure that your lifestyle support emotional health. Ensure that you consume foods that are rich in essential vitamins and minerals. This will promote brain health and help you stabilize your emotions. Another aspect of improving your lifestyle involves cutting out alcohol and toxic substances from your diet. In the western world, so many people are ensnared in alcoholism, and it reduces their capacity to function as normal citizens. When you reduce – or cut out – alcohol intake, you will not only be both physically and emotionally stable, but also, you will do great justice to your wallet.

- **Hang out with the right crowd**

Birds of a feather flock together. When you spend a lot of time with a certain crowd, you end up acquiring their traits. For a person who's into practicing patience, you want to stay with positive individuals. Thus, be careful of whom you let into your life. Seek relations with people who have a positive mindset and are not slaves to negative addictions. Having friends who have a positive mindset will not only promote your capacity to be patient, but it will also accelerate success, considering that you have a ready network to make use of.

METHODS OF BOOSTING CREATIVITY

EMOTIONAL INTELLIGENCE AND CREATIVITY GO HAND IN hand. But most people underutilize their creativity, which is really a great disservice. Creativity is like a muscle, and it has to be exercised on the regular and pushed out of its comfort zone in order to be utilized to the maximum. The following are some important tactics to boost creativity.

- **Collaborate with others**

There's something about cooperating with other people that brings out the best in us. Collaborating with others is about sharing your ideas and listening to the ideas of others. Most successful companies tend to utilize this model in order to come up with world-changing products. The late Steve Jobs, the co-founder of Apple Inc., had a tremendous liking for group work and often said that every major achievement is the work of a group, not individuals. If you learn to collaborate with other people, you will have access to limitless ideas that you can make tweaks on and pass off as yours. But then in as much as working with other people allows you to access many ideas, you have to be careful that you don't ruin your reputation by taking advantage of other people's intellectual property.

- **Do something that you are passionate about**

There's no formula for determining what you are passionate about. But the thing is, once you come across an activity that you are really into, it will make your heart feel to be in the right place. You will be simply ecstatic about it. When you work with something that you are passionate about you are likely to think about it constantly, and this will lead you into a spring of creative ideas. On the contrary, when you work with something that you are not passionate about, it will discourage you from thinking hard upon the matter, and in the end, you won't have many creative ideas to rely on. It is extremely important to have overflowing ideas about a subject so that you may fuse these ideas together and create something worthwhile.

- **Gain inspiration from your superiors**

It doesn't matter what's your line of work. There'll always be people who came there long before you. For instance, if you are in the fashion industry, already there are millions of established names to gain inspiration from. Sometimes, you may have to look out your industry to gain inspiration. There's nothing wrong with that. In fact, it helps to have a "different" approach to your creations, provided that the end result is something that the target audience can relate with. It doesn't matter where you gain inspiration as long as you can tweak these ideas into something that pique's people's interest.

- **Take a rest**

Creativity consumes a lot of mental energy. So what happens when you work for more than necessary, you end up depleting your mental energy. And then from there moving forward, you are not in a position to create something of superior quality, which can cause people to doubt your competency. The world is extremely competitive. And people are not interested in the backstory. So, it is upon you to realize when you have run out of steam and take a rest. When you rest, you allow yourself to be reenergized and feel whole again. You regain the mental energy to keep churning out quality ideas. And this helps you be consistent not just in output but also quality.

- **Take a walk**

The creative process is more often than not turbulent. Most creative people tend to have very stormy minds. But then you must learn to regulate the storms in your mind lest they become a liability. One of the ways you can achieve this is through going for walks. You may find a quiet park or a pavement and make it a ritual. Quiet walks in the evening not only rid you of the stress, but they also promote physical health. Spending time in nature is also great for your spiritual health as the frequencies of the natural world can clear out negative blockages.

- **Boost your mood**

Sometimes you may need a little stimulation before you indulge in the work before you. This is called enhancing the mood. There are many things you could do to set the right mood. For instance, you could improve the decorations of your house, put on some relaxing music, and work on the lighting. For the most part, the best mood enhancer is music. Putting on some relaxing music will help you get into the zone, and this helps you come up with very inspired ideas.

- **Don't be afraid of starting over**

Sometimes working on a concept is not an easy thing. You can easily get lost and become confused. But then instead of trying to find out where you lost your way, it is far much better to start over. When you start over, you will increase your understanding and have special insight.

- **Ask for help**

There's nothing wrong with seeking help whenever you are stuck. If you know an industry leader that you have cordial relations with, you can make a point of reaching out to them and asking for help. Thanks to the internet, nobody can say that they have no channel of receiving help at all. It doesn't matter what your line of work is. There's going to be a forum or a group of like-minded people who are ready to help you. But, of course, you have to approach them with decorum.

- **Ask for feedback**

As a creative person, you will have many instances where you create something that you think is incredible, only to have some people trash it – and for good reasons. And then you will have moments that you create something that you think is terrible and then some other people will consider it outstanding. This means that you cannot solely tell whether something is of superior or inferior quality. Of course, this is a deeply subjective matter, but it helps to hear the opinions of other people. So, don't be afraid to ask people to provide feedback for your creations. Of course, you may attract the wrong type of feedback – negative criticism – but that shouldn't derail you from your main objective.

- **Meditate**

Many successful people have confessed to using meditation as a form of boosting their creativity. Modern existence is no joke. There's a lot happening within a short period of time. And this causes you to have a lot of noise inside of your mind. Meditation is a relaxation exercise that helps you get rid of this noise. And once the noise is eliminated, you are in a position to think clearly. Meditation, without a doubt, promotes creativity.

- **Improve your sleep quality**

If you're running around for the most part of your day, jumping into bed late at night, and waking up after three hours of sleep to start running around again, you can be sure that you will stifle your creative side. The thing about creativity is that it works when you are in a relaxed state of mind. One of the things that will put you in a relaxed state of mind is quality sleep. So, ensure that every night, you are getting adequate sleep. You will have sufficient mental energy to form powerful and creative ideas.

- **Socialize**

Just because you are involved in creating something doesn't mean that you should shun the world. Ensure that you create time to meet up with friends and family. Human beings are social creatures, and we depend on each other to satisfy our emotional needs. Spending time with our friends and relatives helps us to get into a relaxed state of mind. And it is this state of mind that promotes creativity.

- **Exercise**

You don't want to be the sort of person that hardly ever moves out of their chair as they squint at their computer. Exercising is great for you and also for your ambition. It's not a must that you join an expensive gym in order to get started in exercising. There are many exercises that you can perform freehand. If you don't know how to perform certain exercises, you can always watch YouTube and see how to go about it. By exercising, you will improve your mental health and become great at what you do. Exercising will also improve your physical health.

- **Challenge yourself**

When you do just one thing for quite a long time, it will stop challenging you, and sometimes even become a bore, putting you in a docile plane. You should be able to challenge yourself constantly. Once you have achieved a milestone, move on to the next thing.

This is the kind of mentality that promotes growth. But too many people are content with being average. They don't stretch themselves out. And considering that creativity is like a muscle that needs to be constantly exercised, their inactivity causes their creativity to experience the equivalent of atrophy.

TIPS FOR BUILDING CURIOSITY

When we talk of a curious person, we talk about someone who has a sharp eye for detail. They notice various things that escape the average eye. And for that reason, the mind of a curious person is always buzzing with activity, as they try to figure out something. Curiosity is a major force inside every one of us as it bolsters our survival instinct. Emotionally intelligent people tend to be curious. Is it important to be curious? Yes!

Benefits of being curious:

1. It helps us survive: for instance, when you walk into a dark alley, aren't you ever curious? Of course, you are. You want to find out whether there's a monster of a criminal lurking in the shadows that might threaten your life. And this is what causes you to tread with a lot of care. A curious mind is always aware of the various things that might threaten their safety. And such a habit ensures that you get away from dangerous situations.

2. It increases happiness: studies show that curious people are on

average happier than non-curious people. Their happiness stems from the fact that they are interested in many aspects of life. The average person might easily get bored with life because they only notice what is obvious. But the curious person has laser-focus eyes that go beyond the obvious. And this helps them to savor the hidden pleasures of life. Curious people are likely to hold uncommon and seemingly eccentric views about life.

3. It promotes success: the easiest way to achieve success is through capitalizing on a gap. But then most gaps are not obvious. It takes a curious mind to investigate various markets and realize that there's potential along a certain line of work. Thus, curious people can always spot opportunities where average people wouldn't. Also, curiosity helps a person develop their ideas with minimal errors.

4. It promotes empathy: an empathetic person has the capacity to feel what other people are going through. Empathetic can identify with people who are hurting and step in to offer help. But then the capacity to identify those who are hurting is driven by a curious mind. And the world would be a much better place if people were empathetic toward each other, which is sadly not the case.

5. Strengthens relationships: if the parties to a relationship are not perceptive to change, they could easily fall out. Relationship dynamics are complex. And that's why it's necessary to have a sharp eye for what's really going on. In that sense, curiosity helps solve far too many issues, thus mending relationships.

Ways of building curiosity:

- **Break from routine**

The purpose of breaking from routine is to see life from a different angle. If you have been doing a thing in a certain way, now start doing the opposite or the alternative. In this way, you will have an increased perception of various things around you. Breaking from routine certainly helps you become much more curious.

- **Start writing down your ideas**

Another way of increasing your curiosity is through noting down your ideas in a list. If you have anything that you want to try out just note it down. Such a process will give you an insight into the workings of your mind. You will get to see how your mind processes information and understand some of your hidden desires. Above all, it will allow you to see the quirkiness of your mind, which can certainly be interrogated.

- **Get rid of distractions**

In the modern world, there are many things that can hinder us from being attentive. These distractions are mainly tech gadgets and intrusion by people. The young generation is especially affected by tech. They are unlikely to turn their attention away from their phones regardless of what they are doing. And as you can imagine, this denies them the capacity to process their environment well. So, how about getting rid of these distractions and spending some time looking into your life and the environment around you. You will pleasantly arouse your curiosity.

- **Go to a fun event**

Going out to a fun event is another way of increasing your curiosity. It allows you to see life from a bright side. It allows you to investigate people – and even yourself – when they are most happy. Some of the fun events that you can attend include, dancing shows, movie theaters, and festivals.

- **Get into books**

One of the ways to increase your curiosity is through reading books. When you read books, you are exposed to different ways of thought. It challenges your thinking process. And this leads to the acquisition of more knowledge. Someone who's used to reading books tends to have a superior way of thinking, and they also have a tendency of being curious. Reading books also boosts your creative side and makes you a problem-solver.

- **Watch people**

Sometimes, the easiest way to understand yourself is by figuring out people. One of the things you can do to try to figure out various things about people is by watching how they behave. So, make a habit of watching people as they go on with their lives, and you'll be surprised at the number of things you learn. You might sit in a park and watch the world go around. Of course, it won't answer all the questions you may have, but it will give you some perspective.

- **Approach strangers**

If you want to develop your curious nature, you have to start talking to people that you have ties with. This means walking up to strangers and striking conversations. It can be nerve-wracking in the beginning, but as you practice, it becomes easy. People don't necessarily hold similar views or attitudes toward life. And holding conversations with different people should spark your curiosity.

- **Learn a new skill**

Do your research and identify a skill that you would love having except you haven't got the time to develop it. And then make a commitment toward developing it. Learning a new skill will help you acquire a new perspective on the related field and bring out your curiosity. Thanks to the internet, you don't have to fork out large school fees anymore, as you can acquire new skills through YouTube and cheap online courses.

- **Travel**

Nothing fills up the mind with questions and ideas more than traveling in different places. You get to see different cultures and people. Traveling, both domestic and internationally is not necessarily expensive. You just have to look for bargains and ensure that you travel light and live like an average life in new destinations. So, start saving now so that you may travel the world.

- **Connect with average people**

If you are one of the lucky ones who have had a sheltered life, mom and daddy have hidden you from many realities. So, how about finding out for yourself what this is about. In order to start identifying with the common man, you have to live as they do. So, get into the habit of mixing with average people, eating out at their restaurants, and living an average life. It will show you a side to life that you had not previously been aware of.

- **Learn new topics one at a time**

In order to maximize your perceptive power, you want to concentrate on one topic at a time. Thus, ensure that you learn about one topic before you move on to the next. This will boost your capacity to question various things. If you are interested in many topics at the same time, your attention would be divided, and you wouldn't be perceptive enough.

- **Ask questions**

One of the ways to boost curiosity is by asking questions. Just keep them coming as though you were a small girl. The thing about questions is that they give you new perspectives.

- **Start taking photos**

Another way of increasing your curiosity is through taking photos. This will help you notice details to a thing or person that would previously go unnoticed. A good photographer must be big on focus, and as a result, you start noticing more things in your daily life. If you develop your skill extremely well, who says that you shouldn't commercially? So, sign up for those stock image memberships sites and make a buck from your photos.

- **Become an active listener**

It's a bit hard for the average person to listen actively. They have to battle against distractions both in their mind and around them. But being an active listener is vital for developing your curiosity. This is simply because our perceptions are informed by what we hear.

So, if we can hear everything that the person says, it literally means we have more stuff to be curious about. But if we are not listening actively, we risk letting our minds modify what we think we have heard, and it stalls our capacity to be curious. So, what does active listening entail? You should face the other person squarely, assume an erect posture, get rid of distractions, and maintain eye contact.

TIPS FOR MASTERING YOUR EMOTIONS

EMOTIONS ARE POWERFUL FORCES, AND UNLESS YOU ARE skilled at handling them, you are at risk of getting burned. But then handling emotions is not rocket science. If you commit yourself to understanding your emotions, you can capitalize on it. The following tips are designed to help you master your emotions.

- **Observe your feelings**

Most of us seem unable to observe our emotions and what we are good at is simply acting them out. It takes discipline to be able to take the role of the observer where your emotions are concerned. Set some time during the day where you observe your emotional temperature. When you are aware of your emotions, you are less likely to fall into the trap of being negatively influenced by these emotions while making critical decisions like selecting a marriage partner, investment partner, or even spending.

- **Observe your behaviors**

Is it possible for someone to be unaware of how they are acting? Yes! Your unconscious mind causes you to display manners that relate to your emotional state. Thus, you have to take care that you are not displaying the wrong behaviors. Take some time every day to study your behaviors. This will help you understand the range of your behaviors in relation to your emotional statuses.

- **Question your own convictions**

Don't be happy that you are part of a group. Instead, ask yourself precisely why you hold a similar opinion as that group. Is it because of your volatile emotions? Is it because of the influence of your close friend? What is it? Asking yourself these questions will help you see the role of your emotions in developing opinions.

- **Accept responsibility for your emotions**

Unless you are an empath – someone who absorbs the emotions of those around them – you have no business blaming anybody else for the emotions you are experiencing. Understand that those emotions are the sum result of your decisions. And you made those decisions. The reason why it's important to take responsibility for your emotional states is that it inspires you to take a proactive approach to develop your emotional intelligence.

- **Celebrate your wins**

As you gather pace toward success, understand that you have an ally in the name your subconscious mind. Your subconscious mind monitors your goals and verifies whether these goals come true or not. If the goals come true, your subconscious becomes your ally, but if you fail, your subconscious mind starts doubting whether you are fit for success. So, set achievable goals, and every time you achieve, celebrate.

- **Focus on the bright side but don't ignore the negative**

Always keep your eyes on the positive side of things. It will help you to have a staying power. Of course, such a mentality won't save you from bad things actually happening. But then ensure that you are always sticking to the positive. Does this mean that you should ignore the negative side? By no means! At the end of the day, you are a human being and prone to fault. Embrace your faults and move on. And also look for corrective measures against your weaknesses and faults.

- **Deep-breathing exercises**

When you are overwhelmed with emotions, it can be pretty hard to focus, thus affecting your productivity. In such times, you may want to practice the deep-breathing exercise. It involves taking a seat in a comfortable place and assuming an erect posture. And then you may breathe in and out in a slow fashion as you cast away the negative energies. This exercise will improve not only your emotional health but also your physical health.

- **Capitalize on your strengths**

God never intended us to be superhuman. And that's why he created us with both strengths and weaknesses. In order to go far in life, you must learn how to capitalize on your strengths. For instance, if you are exceedingly strong, but poor in aesthetics, it would be wise to follow a career in contact sports and not a career in fashion or TV. When you capitalize on your strengths, you are likely to prosper, and it will improve your emotional health.

- **Keep a diary**

Note down the various things that are taking place in your life. Also, note down your thoughts. A diary helps a person capture their precise emotional nature. It helps one observe their quirky traits. Ensure that you write your diary with a lot of honesty so that you can be able to track patterns appropriately.

- **Understand your motivations**

Every person who's looking to achieve a certain goal has a reason. It's called motivation. So, if you are working toward a goal, there must be something that motivates you too. It would be great to identify your motivating factor. When the going gets tough, as it normally does, you will remind yourself of why you began in the first place.

- **Know your emotional triggers**

Every person has an emotional trigger. It's basically the thing that causes you to experience negative emotions. If you had a traumatic childhood, say your uncle took advantage of you, now years later you may be having occasional grief when you run into anything that remotely reminds you of your uncle. Ensure that you have down all the things that trigger your emotions.

- **Develop your intuitive side**

Being intuitive refers to an individual's capability to perceive things long before there's evidence. For instance, Donald Trump, 45th President of the US, relies on his gut feeling to gauge whether a deal is good or not. Studies show that this force can be incredibly helpful when it comes to making the right decisions.

- **Follow a schedule**

If there's no structure to your life, you are unnecessarily wasting a ton of time, making poor decisions, and in the process ruining your emotional health. Ensure that your day is structured. This enables you to know what you must be doing at every moment of the day. And it discourages time wastage.

- **Have a balanced diet**

Many studies show that there's a link between a person's diet and their emotional state. If someone is stuck on a bad diet, they are likely to have a negative emotional state; it happens indirectly. A poor diet usually causes one to become overweight. And then the excess kilos cause the person to have a low opinion of themselves, thus inviting depression and anxiety. On the other hand, a great diet causes one to improve their looks and get fit. And, in turn, they feel great about themselves. Emotional intelligence promotes healthy feelings.

- **Stop having expectations**

The easiest way to get frustrated with life is through having lofty expectations, especially on matters that you have no control over. If someone promises to do something, don't obsess over it but, actually, detach. If they live to their promise great, and if they don't, that's too bad. But when you stop having expectations about people, you will save yourself needless emotional turmoil.

- **Create goals**

The purpose of being emotionally intelligent is to help you make the right choices in life and attain success faster than you thought possible, but for that to happen, you have to be focused. And nothing makes you more focused than having a goal. It has to be an attainable goal. It gives meaning to your hard work. So, always create achievable goals and break them down.

- **Have a mentor**

Scaling the heights of success comes at a cost. You have to be willing to take various measures. One of these measures is securing a mentor. This is someone who's probably been where you are, and they lived to attain success. This must be someone that you look up to. Ensure that you have someone to mentor you into a successful person.

- **Avoid being proud**

Success doesn't happen within a vacuum. You will succeed in front of other people. But, most importantly, you will succeed through the help of other people. No one is ever self-made. And that's why you must avoid displaying dark personality traits like excessive self-praise and pride. Such dark behaviors turn people away from you as you are obviously a nasty character. And in the event that you still succeed even as everyone shuns you, people may not give you respect, which hurts.

- **Be a good listener**

Good listening skills are indicative of emotional intelligence. Be that person who's fully focused when another person is talking to you. Being a good listener is about keeping your body language right. It minimizes chances of miscommunication, and it also encourages the speaker. It never hurts to have cordial relations with other people.

- **Improve your social skills**

If you are fond of apologizing to other people in social situations saying that you are a shy person, you need to stop saying that and actually develop your social skills. Being shy will cause you to make self-inhibiting decisions, which is not a cute thing. Improving your social skills takes work, I won't lie to you, but in the end, the effort is every bit worth the results. Having great social skills allows you to go out there, meet people, start relationships, which does a world of good to your emotional health.

CAREERS FOR PEOPLE WITH HIGH EMOTIONAL INTELLIGENCE

RECENT STUDIES HAVE SHOWN THAT EMOTIONAL QUOTIENT IS far important that intelligent quotient. People who are in control of their emotions and know how to react to the emotions of other people stand a far greater chance at success than anybody else. These are some of the careers that people with high emotional intelligence seem to thrive.

- **Marketing manager**

Marketing in today's world is a far cry from what it used to be. In the days of long ago, there were small channels of communication, and there were rules to marketing. But in the modern world, there are almost no rules, and the channels are far too many. It really depends on the nature of your clientele. If you are targeting kids and young adults, you want to market through social media, but if you are targeting adult audiences, you may still have to purchase TV adverts. A marketing manager oversees the running of an agency, and they have to be sharp with decisions so that they can utilize the resources to the maximum. A marketing manager should be able to create an environment that allows creativity to thrive.

- **Lawyers**

As long as human beings are around, crimes will continue to be committed. Lawyers are the people who defend alleged wrongdoers in a court of law. They can also be hired by people who believe they have been done wrong and are seeking legal remedy. Lawyers play a critical role in promoting the smooth running of society. But then in order to be a great lawyer, you have to have a significantly high emotional intelligence, not to mention sharp communication skills. This is what will help you argue your case very well and help your client win the case. Lawyers have to have great people skills too.

- **Sales managers**

Studies show that sales managers play an important role in attracting customers. Simply because a business is offering a particular product or service won't make every potential customer throw money at them. It takes proper talks between a sales manager and potential customers to strike a deal that will see the transaction effected. A sales manager needs to have the capacity to read into the emotions of their customers and tell them what they need to hear. They also have to have a great capacity to control their emotions. This is because whatever the customer will be saying won't necessarily be rosy. And when the sales manager fumes at customers, he risks losing business.

- **Events planner**

Nowadays, people are so into creating celebrations. For that reason, an events planner is in high demand. Whether it's planning a party, wedding, or a corporate event, the events planner must coordinate various aspects in order to ensure the party or event is successful. Events planners tend to work with various people, and they have to be skilled at making quick decisions. Event planners must have high emotional intelligence because there's the potential for sudden changes. You never what's coming. And whenever plans change, instead of despairing, they should adjust pretty quickly. Event planners need to be great at handling people too.

- **General operations manager**

Nowadays, a company doesn't have to post hundreds of millions in profits in order to have an operations manager. There's a need to have a manager that oversees the smooth running of the company. The ideal candidate must have great communication skills, not to mention that they must have the capacity to listen to the needs of the employers and find solutions as quickly as possible. A person with low emotional intelligence would easily become drained by this kind of work. The operations manager must also cater to the requests of customers and monitor how the company performs in comparison with other companies of its class.

- **Academic administrator**

These are the sort of jobs that never go out of style. I mean, there will always be people going to school. But in order to succeed with such a job, you have to be one of a kind. You have to be excellent at reading the minds of students and realizing how you can modify their programs in order to make the most impact in their lives. An education administrator is the central link between students, parents, and the administration. They are well aware of must be done in order to achieve certain goals. Education must have a high emotional intelligence else they would be unable to cope with the many demands of the job.

- **Assistants of physicians**

When we think of physicians, we think of them as gods considering that patients are at their mercy. But there are some important workers that we seem to ignore. Physician assistants: they streamline the work for the physician so as to eliminate confusion and to ensure that sessions progress with minimal or zero distraction. Physician assistants have to have high emotional intelligence so that they can accommodate the needs of both the physician and the patient. The nature of their job demands that they are alert because a patient's recovery process is not always linear. Also, in their line of work, they get to see human beings at their weakest, and it takes emotional intelligence not to let that bother you.

- **Construction directors**

Since housing is a basic need, there'll always be demand for houses. If you intend to erect a great house in the city or in the country, you may want to contact a construction manager. These people will answer all the questions you have concerning building a house – whether for private use or commercial purposes. In the modern world, there's an ever-increasing demand for houses because of domestic and international migration into cities. But then in order to be successful at this sort of work, you have to have an exceedingly high emotional intelligence. It's about meeting people from various backgrounds with rigid beliefs, absurd demands, and it can be hard to guide them into the light. Also, you may fail to meet the expectations of your clients, which would amount to heartbreak if you weren't emotionally intelligent.

- **Movie directors**

Have you ever taken a look into the massive amount of money that action movies make? Well, it takes a good director to make a good movie that will net the studio hundreds of millions – sometimes billions – in sales. But being a movie director is no walk in the park. You will have to deal with dozens of people with an inflated sense of worth and make them toe the line. It's not an easy job. You not only need to have high emotional intelligence, but you also need to have assertive skills, great communication skills, and unshakable self-confidence. At the end of the day, you are the captain, and the buck stops with you.

- **Physical trainer**

A physical trainer helps their clients become physically fit. Maybe the client is struggling with obesity or some life-threatening disease, and they need coaching so that they can get their life back together. The physical trainer needs to listen to the needs of the client, and every decision they make must have a positive impact. The comfort of a physical trainer is solely in the hands of the client. If they run into a client with a bad attitude, the physical trainer will be disturbed, and consider even asking away the client, but if they meet a considerate client, then everything seems to fall into place. Some people ask why people with lifestyle issues wouldn't do a simple search online and implement the remedies on Google. A physical trainer has consumed all of the information and knows the combination that will work best for different clients. Remember, it's about achieving the desired results within a particular period of time. And clients are willing to pay to minimize the time that it will take to see results.

- **Therapist**

To say that most people in the world are hurting would be an understatement. People are really in a world of pain. But one of the ways of dealing with pain is through seeking a therapist. This is someone who helps you understand the genesis of your pain and how you may reduce or eliminate it altogether. A therapist must be skilled at comprehending the range of emotions that people experience. Also, they must have high emotional intelligence so that they can understand where their clients are coming from and what sort of remedy best suits them. Sometimes it can be difficult to handle the expectations of clients who probably expect a magic bullet that will heal all of their troubles as opposed to taking the long, hard route of recovery.

HABITS OF EMOTIONALLY HEALTHY PEOPLE

When we talk about emotionally healthy people, we are talking about people who are mentally tough. They are unafraid of expressing themselves even if it means inviting criticism. Emotionally healthy people will always move forward despite their challenges. The following are some of the habits that emotionally healthy people display.

- **They walk tall**

Emotionally intelligent people don't hang their heads, I shame while they are walking out in public. Instead, they hold their heads high; as they know that they are enough. An emotionally healthy person is not looking for acceptance from other people, and he's looking to make his mark while he respects other people. But then they are careful not to come off as arrogant or proud. Emotionally healthy people have sufficient confidence, but they don't use it as a weapon for hurting others, but rather, they use it to uplift and inspire people.

- **They know how to handle toxic people**

Emotionally healthy people are not scared of toxic people. But they know how to handle them. They are aware that toxic people are looking for a showdown, but they deny them that. Emotionally healthy people will allow toxic people to express themselves, and then, they'll answer in the calmest manner. Also, they let the toxic people realize that they want to understand them and make peace. When a toxic person encounters an emotionally intelligent person, they are bound to be humbled as things progress in a way they hadn't expected.

- **They are not afraid of change**

Emotionally intelligent people understand that change is a constant factor. For that reason, emotionally intelligent people welcome change instead of fighting it. They are good at adapting to changes too. On the other hand, people who are not emotionally intelligent tend to fight change, and ultimately, they lose. Flexibility is a vital skill in the journey to success. There will always be new factors coming into play, and those who are wise enough to adapt will gain the most. Emotionally intelligent people are not only good at adapting to change, but also, they keep a good attitude while welcoming change.

- **They are not afraid of saying, "No."**

Emotionally intelligent people have no qualms about helping out when the circumstances are right. However, if they are not in a position to help, they won't hesitate to say "No." Emotionally intelligent people understand that saying "No" is about making the best use of their time, and it's never done in good faith. Of course, not everyone will receive "No" in good faith. Some people may develop a bad attitude after being told "No" and start negative criticism. But then the emotionally intelligent person is not fazed by negative criticism.

- **They confront their fears**

The average person tries as much as they can to steer clear of what they are afraid of. But the emotionally intelligent person actually confronts their fears. For instance, if they have a business idea, but they develop a fear that the idea might fail, they start the business anyway. Emotionally intelligent people know too well that success is on the other end of the tunnel known as fear. They know that if they can harden themselves and meet their fears, they can be able to scale the heights of success.

- **They seek apology when they wrong someone**

Emotionally healthy people understand that asking for forgiveness after wronging someone is a sign of strength, not weakness. They are careful not to go around looking for fights. They understand that keeping good relationships between people is vital for success. On the other hand, emotionally unintelligent people believe that offending people and not apologizing is a mark of strength. They have a twisted sense of seeking glory. In the end, the emotionally intelligent person wins people's admiration because of their maturity while the emotionally unintelligent person receives ridicule.

- **They get adequate sleep**

Emotionally intelligent people understand that hard work is critical for success. But in the same breath, hard work doesn't amount to denying yourself sleep. These people understand the value of getting enough sleep. It will revitalize them and prepare them to get started for the day.

- **They watch what they eat**

Emotionally intelligent people are great at watching what goes into their stomach. They understand that having a balanced diet is the key to improving their physical health as well as their looks. Thus, emotionally intelligent people invest a lot in their diet. On the other hand, emotionally unintelligent people don't really care about what they consume.

- **They socialize**

Emotionally intelligent people understand that it is important to start great relationships with other people. For that reason, they are not afraid of approaching people and striking conversations. Emotionally intelligent people have great social skills that help them carry on conversations pretty well. They are not scared of meeting new people and expanding their network.

- **They read books**

Emotionally intelligent people have a habit of reading books. They are well aware that this is the only way of increasing their knowledge. So, they make reading books a hobby. They are not biased against one topic because they understand that inspiration can stem from any background. Of course, they may have a favorite genre, but it doesn't stop them from reading books touching on a variety of areas.

- **They avoid debt**

Emotionally healthy people tend to live within their means. After all, they are not looking to impress anyone and spend money aimlessly. This mindset allows them to avoid debt. People who are low on emotional intelligence tend to get trapped in debt because of their impulsive spending habits and a need to glorify themselves.

- **They nurture their personal relationships**

Emotionally intelligent people are aware that personal relationships play a critical role in their emotional health. For that reason, they always look to improve their personal relationships. For instance, they may give their significant other a gift, take them on a date, or prepare their favorite dish. They understand that nurturing a relationship is mostly about the small stuff, and not necessarily spending millions to impress their partner.

- **They laugh**

If someone is gloomy at all times, it might mean that they are low on emotional intelligence. Their negative emotions are, in part influenced by their narrow-mindedness. But then someone with high emotional intelligence will have many reasons to laugh about. They don't have to go to a comedy show in order to laugh. The day to day happenings around them are sufficient comedy.

- **They say, "Thank you."**

*E*motionally healthy people recognize people who have helped them by saying, "Thank you." They are grateful. And they don't take people for granted. But someone with low emotional intelligence is unlikely to say "Thank you" when they receive help from someone.

- **They meditate**

Meditation is a relaxation exercise that is vital for washing away energy blockages. Negativity comes to all – the emotionally intelligent and the unintelligent. But then the emotionally intelligent person takes an extra step of meditating so as to clear away the pent up negative energies. The beauty of meditation is that it can be practiced pretty much anywhere. All you have to do is make the area comfortable and become focused.

- **They have a diary**

People who are emotionally healthy know that it is critical to note down important events in their life. For that reason, they keep a diary. They write down all the major things happening in their life and also major thoughts. This helps them gain an understanding of both their emotions and habits.

- **They receive medical checkups**

Not to mean that they have an unrealistic dread for illnesses, but emotionally healthy people are aware that regular checkups are critical for long term prime health. They get checked up on the regular so that if a problem is found, it can be resolved pretty fast.

- **They don't reveal the whole of their life on social media**

Not to mean that they have no use for social media, but rather that they acknowledge the usefulness of social media in keeping in touch with friends and loved ones, and that if not used well it can actually be a liability. One of the things that may count as a poor use of social media is revealing everything – I mean everything – about your life, posting pictures of yourself when you wake up, when you go for lunch, and the photos of your kids, your pets and posting everything and deny yourself any privacy.

- **They forgive others**

Emotionally healthy people apologize when they wrong someone. In the same breath, they forgive those who wrong them. They are about creating peace in life and letting everyone have a great time.

- **They challenge themselves**

Emotionally healthy people are careful not to settle in their comfort zone. They know too well that the comfort zone will cause them to be stagnant. Thus, they have to push themselves to perform well. Emotionally healthy people know too well that hard work is the single most important force of creating success, and they are unafraid of challenging themselves.

WAYS OF DEVELOPING A POSITIVE MINDSET

Emotional intelligence guides a person into developing a positive mindset. Having a positive mindset is critical in the sense that it grants you the staying power, boosts your confidence, and improves your mood. In order to attain success, you must operate with a positive mindset, and shun negativity in all its forms. The following are some of the ways that you may develop a positive mindset.

- **Utilize the power of positive affirmations**

Positive affirmations are short phrases that you chant at the beginning of the day. They are essentially positive messages that go straight into your subconscious mind. Positive affirmations help you breed positivity into your life. Perform your research around the various positive affirmations that you want to use so that they may have a maximum impact on your subconscious mind. When you wake up, chant your positive affirmations, and also chant them at different times throughout the day. When you run into a particularly challenging situation, that's also an opportune moment to chant your positive affirmation, and you will bulk up with positive energy to see you through the challenge.

- **Focus on the bright side**

Understand the fact that things will not always be great. But then, even if you run into problems, that's no excuse for having a negative attitude. In such situations, make a point of looking at the bright side of things. This is an indication of a serious attitude adjustment. It takes a lot of confidence to consider the bright side when you encounter problems. But developing such a habit will help you increase both your fighting spirit and your patience. Nothing worth having ever comes without a struggle. So, ensure that you are always focusing on the things that are going right for you, but at the same time, don't ignore the negative aspects, but rather quietly look for a solution to these challenges.

- **Spot the humor in all situations**

People with high emotional intelligence will always be the first to sense the start of a joke. They laugh before everyone else catches on. Having emotional intelligence causes you to have a mind that processes emotions pretty fast. You get to realize that there's humor in every conceivable situation. The importance of having a funny bone is that it helps wipe off your depressing thoughts and negative energies. It is simply an inexpensive way of receiving therapy for your negative pent up emotions.

- **Turn failure into success**

There's one thing that you must not be afraid of: failure. If you have never failed, it simply means you have never tried to do anything. And that's not cool. In your journey toward success, you may run into failure. But then your reaction will make all the difference. If you decide to label yourself a victim and throw the blame on everyone else, you cannot be helped, but if you decide to turn your failure into success, you won't stay down for long, and you'll actually look for a way forward. Turning failure into success is about conquering your fears and developing the belief that a better day awaits. It helps you to act with faith. And such a mindset helps you achieve your important life goals.

- **Stop the negative self-talk**

One of the reasons why some people hardly ever achieve success is that they are stuck in negative self-talk. They have never seen themselves as deserving of success. For instance, if a big opportunity comes up, you might hear them saying something along the lines of, "I am not good with people. I always botch things up." Such a defeatist mentality prepares them for failure. Having negative self-talk is being unfair to yourself, considering that there are more than enough people out there who have already taken that role. So, stop the negative self-talk and get started on positive self-talk.

- **Put your mind to the present**

Most negative people are either imprisoned by their past or worry excessively about the future. They seem unaware of the fact that focusing on the present is the secret to building a positive mindset. When you are stuck in your past, you can hardly make progress in life as you are consumed by both euphoria and sorrow in an alternating fashion. Learning to focus on the present shouldn't be a hard task. You only have to remind yourself every few hours to shift your focus into the present. Such an attitude will not only help you overcome your challenges but also lead to the development of a strong mindset that will see you fight for your dreams.

- **Keep friends with a positive mindset**

Of course, one of the easiest ways of developing a positive mindset is through keeping positive friends. Remember that we end up becoming like our friends. If we hang out with a crowd of negative people, we are going to become negative ourselves, but if we spend time with positive people, we will become positive ourselves. The importance of keeping positive friends as a method of improving your emotional health is that it is an effortless task. But then you want to ensure that you spend only enough time with these people and not spending more time than necessary.

- **Be purposeful**

Stop making decisions for the sake of it. Ensure that you are deliberate. This will not only help you make the right decisions but also create a sense of direction to your life. Being purposeful is about having a strategy for achieving your important life goals. Thus, you must make decisions with the full understanding of what is likely to become of those decisions. When you are aware of the possible outcomes, you stop being someone that relies on merely luck to get ahead in life, and you become someone that is calculative and has a strategy for scaling the heights of success.

- **Go the extra mile**

Acquiring a positive mindset comes with a bit of a struggle. You never sit around and then suddenly awaken to find yourself with a positive mindset. One of the things you must do is push yourself a little harder. This means you must always exceed expectations. Always give more than you take. And such an attitude is critical in developing a great mindset.

- **Be realistic**

Some people end up bitter and disillusioned simply because their decisions and convictions were inspired by some fantasy as opposed to being rooted in reality. For instance, if you are a scrawny teenager with a lumpy face, you cannot dream of suddenly becoming a male supermodel and scoring acting deals left right and center. A realistic dream would be along the lines of working on your talent, e.g., writing and securing a job with a local magazine.

- **Have allies**

One of the reasons why people have trouble creating a mindset that would help them reach success is down to an inability to connect with other human beings. In other words, they lack a support system. We human beings are social animals, and we need to interact with others in order to improve our emotional health. Having allies helps us create a positive mindset since we have like-minded individuals to offer us support. So, ensure that you have cordial relations with other people.

- **Have a routine**

Some people feel as though a routine would stifle their creativity, but in all honesty, a routine would actually help. When you act without a routine, you are at risk of making poor use of your time. But then a routine allows you to plan your day, to have the most important tasks taken care of, to go for breaks at the opportune moment, and to ensure that you are making the best use of your time. When creating your schedule, you should be a bit flexible so that it allows you to feel free.

- **Stop seeking validation**

As long as you are seeking validation, understand that your priorities and goals are misplaced. People who seek validation from others have zero confidence in themselves, and they must rely on others to feel great. It becomes very easy for other people to manipulate them. In order to stop seeking validation, just ask yourself what's your main motivation. Once you recognize the one thing that motivates you, you will start to disregard sideshows and develop a firm stance in your beliefs. When you stop seeking validation, you will be in a position to develop a positive mindset.

- **Take responsibility**

Emotionally healthy people have one thing in common. They don't run away from responsibility. And this is a clear sign of both maturity and mental toughness. People who run away from responsibilities are nothing more than cowards. When you accept responsibility, you allow yourself to be proactive, but when you run away from responsibility, you take on the role of the victim, which denies you power. Someone with high emotional intelligence will always want to have the power to determine the course of their lives through consistent application of effort. People with high emotional intelligence hardly run away from their responsibilities.

HOW TO INCREASE YOUR WILLPOWER

WHEN WE TALK OF WILLPOWER, WE ARE REFERRING TO AN individual's capacity to keep taking action so that they may achieve a goal that they deeply desire. Someone with strong willpower is not merely patient, but rather, they take relentless action all in a bid to make their dreams come true. Researchers have come out in recent times to claim that willpower is the single most powerful factor of success. Emotionally healthy people tend to have the willpower that sees them aggressively fight for their dreams. One of the best situations to see willpower at work is during a political race for office, especially for the presidency. That's when you see people bringing out their relentless willpower as they seek to accomplish their goal of becoming president. Research also shows that willpower can actually be improved through consistent practice. The following measures help people to develop their willpower.

- **The power of music**

Sometimes you only require the right music in order to keep your fighting spirit up. Whenever you are performing an important activity, ensure that you have some light music in the background. Thanks to enhanced moods, you will be in a position to fortify your willpower and get started on transforming your life. Stress pops up from all corners. But listening to inspiring music tends to fight away the stress and allows us to become strong-willed warriors as we look to make our dreams come true. The definition of inspiring music varies from one person to another. But, all in all, the importance of music in forming great willpower cannot be overstated.

- **Stop encouraging clichés**

As you fight for your dreams, the idea is that you are scaling your way to the summit of success, yes, but then you have to discourage various thoughts such as trying to hit the peak. Someone with sufficient willpower hardly ever settles. As soon as they acquire something, they'll quickly get started on the next challenge, and it never ends. On the other hand, someone with a low emotional quotient will aim for a particular goal, and once they achieve that goal, they will cling to it fiercely, so that their entire life will revolve around that goal.

- **Quality sleep**

Research shows that people who get quality sleep tend to have great self-discipline. To some extent, having willpower is akin to being disciplined, except that you are proactive about reaching your important life goals and turning your life around. Getting quality sleep every night will help you strengthen your willpower. Quality sleep may vary from person to person, but ideally, it involves sleeping in a comfortable bed with the lights off and at favorable temperature. This force, known as willpower, doesn't spring from thin air, but you have to actually develop it.

- **Play games**

Studies have shown that people who play strategy games have a far better chance of increasing their willpower. Strategy games call on the player to utilize their mental resources and find a solution. As you race toward your goal, understand that you will run into hardship from time to time, but instead of despairing, you may elect to play strategy games if only to entertain oneself if not to stack up on willpower. Nowadays, there is easy access to these games, considering that the internet is affordable.

- **Stop skipping meals**

Some people skip meals for various reasons: watching weight, improving body aesthetics, etc. But such an approach is actually retrogressive. Skipping meals will only mess your emotions up and weaken your capacity to exercise your willpower. If you are interested in improving your health, there are various other ways you may do that without skipping meals. For instance, you could start a diet, calorie counting, or increase the intensity of your physical training. When you stop skipping meals, you will have sufficient willpower to keep fighting for your dreams.

- **Clean your living space**

Staying in a clean environment can boost your willpower. On the other hand, being surrounded by a mess and having the whole area disorganized can actually weaken your willpower. To avoid falling victim to mess and disorganization, ensure that your living space is always clean. This will promote good mental health, and it will help you lead a productive life.

- **Use the phrase "I will" in your goals**

At the end of the day, having willpower is about having incredible self-belief. It doesn't matter what you are up against, but you believe that you are up to the task. Saying "I will" puts you in the right emotional mindset. It's a way of psyching yourself up for success. When creating goals, ensure that you use this phrase "I will" as it will help you get into the mindset of success. This mindset is critical in achieving success, and it also discourages you from blaming others when you come short of your expectations.

- **Mindfulness**

Your willpower can also benefit from a concept known as mindfulness. This is where you focus your energy upon the things that are taking place in your life and at the present moment. Willpower is a form of energy. And if we misuse this energy, we stand to lose. One of the ways to safeguard this energy is through savoring the present moment and detaching yourself from the heavy challenges of the world. By practicing mindfulness, you increase your chances of being a resourceful person who will stay unbowed, fighting for your dreams, until you attain your goals in a successive fashion.

- **Rely on routines**

One of the advantages of routines is the fact that they save us from making constant decisions. Create a routine that allows you to perform the most important work and, at the same time, spare you of constant decisions. There's something known as decision fatigue, and it has a real negative effect on a person's willpower.

- **Be a little controversial**

If you are just another person who wants to achieve a certain goal despite the odds not being in your favor, there's nothing special about that. But if you spice things up by causing some controversies, you will actually attract attention, and your willpower, if anything, will receive a boost.

HOW TO STOP BEING LAZY

If there's a major enemy to emotional intelligence, it has got to be laziness. A lazy person can never be emotionally intelligent because they lack discipline. But then laziness is not a curse. It's something you can overcome quite easily. And once you overcome laziness, you get started on the path to a fruitful life. The following are some of the techniques you might want to incorporate in your fight against laziness.

- **Find a compelling, motivating factor**

Before you decide to leave your lazy ways behind and focus on turning your life around, you will need a good enough reason to do that. And this reason shouldn't be as vague as to say, "I want to become rich." Having a strong motivating factor is about being strongly convinced about what you want to do. For instance, you might say, "I want to stop wasting time and actually get a part-time job so that I can help my parents with the bills." Such a statement would be a strong reason why you want to stop sleeping the entire day as the world moves ahead. It has to be a strong enough reason or else it won't move you into action.

- **Take a step at a time**

When you have discovered the magic of a force known as hard work, you may be tempted to overwork yourself. But then that would be counteractive. The trick is to take one step at a time. By taking one step at a time, you are sure that you are making the right decisions considering that you are not overwhelmed. On the other hand, when you have a tendency of handling two or more tasks at the same time, you invite the possibility for making an error, and if you carry on with this trend, you run out of steam and go back to your previous unsavory self.

- **Exercise**

The fact that you care to spend some energy in a workout session is a good place to start. There's a host of physical and mental health benefits to exercising. When you awaken from sleep, put on your training shoes and head to the gym. A workout session should get you all sweaty, but don't worry about the energy you have spent there, for you will be invigorated, and have many times over more energy. Exercising is a sure way of getting rid of laziness as it gives you emotional and physical strength. But then you have to take to exercising on the regular for you to spot the considerable difference.

- **Divvy up your tasks**

Assume that you are a sales manager, and you open your laptop to find pages of unrecorded data spanning months, and you have to complete that assignment in a few days, what would you do? Wouldn't you lose enthusiasm and just close your computer and start fantasizing? Or maybe you would sit down and start typing up anyway. But then you miss the point. You could very well split up the assignment into smaller milestones and work on these milestones one by one. Such an approach is far easier as it allows you to take the amounts of work you are comfortable handling.

- **Look for inspiration**

The easiest way to stop being a bag of lazy bones is to identify a positive influence in your life, whether they are within your reach or they exist in faraway lands, and you have formed a relationship with them through TV and computers. When it comes to selecting the person or thing that inspires you most, you don't have to go for the biggest name out there just for the sake of it, but stick to someone that you are genuinely impressed with. For instance, they may be a reformed alcoholic who's improving their relationship with Jesus. If you are fighting addiction, you should consider such a person as your inspiration.

- **Remind yourself of the consequences**

Another incredible way of fighting off your laziness is through realizing the consequences. Of course, no one is fond of consequences, but when you think hard about them, you realize the need to stop your laziness and work anyway. For instance, if you are employed as a researcher, and for some crazy reason, you find that job a mixture of difficult and boring, you might become lazy and start slacking. But then such an attitude would put you in legal trouble, and you might also lose your job. Realizing the consequences of your actions – e.g., losing your job – might cause you to get rid of laziness and improve your quality output.

- **Visualization**

When we talk of visualization, we are talking of an individual's capacity to visualize themselves as they do a particular task and then going ahead to do it. This technique is especially rewarding in cases where someone believes that a task is too difficult. In order to improve your visualization skills, you will have to invest in your mental energy. Visualization will not only boost your resistance to laziness, but also, it will spark your creativity. This means that you get to work with an inspired zeal. Many successful people have admitted to using this technique to overcome their challenges and scale the heights of success.

- **Set deadline on yourself**

Deadlines can be a huge bore. They unconsciously remind us of the big man syndrome and stir our rebelliousness unconsciously. But then you must admit that deadlines are to an extent effective in getting someone – lazy bones – actually to do something. Merely noting the deadline can inspire you to take action. If you are lazy and you need to take action at that instant, you may want to start counting down, and at the end of the countdown, you are to perform that task. Imposing deadlines on yourself might feel like torture, but this technique actually works when it comes to dragging you out of laziness.

- **Surround yourself with hard working people**

As they say, birds of a feather flock together. So, if you mean to overcome your laziness, become a productive member of society, you may have to surround yourself with the right crowd. At the end of the day, we gain the traits of those that we spend the most time with. If they are arrogant and lazy cows, we will become just as they are, and if they are hardworking men of valor, we will also absorb those great benefits. Considering that humans are discriminative, you may have an extreme challenge meeting a pack that will accept you with your flaws, but then the answer is always to have a determined spirit.

- **Improve your environment**

If your house looks like a dumpster and nothing is located where it should, you are likely to be lazy yourself. You can overcome this challenge by sprucing up your house and making it a sweet haven. Once you have retouched your house, the organized structure of your house gives you the peace of mind to pursue other interests.

- **Handle the difficult tasks at the opportune time**

Since you are the one who understands yourself best, you know at what time of day you are literally overflowing with energy. So, this is the time that you handle the most difficult task. And then you can handle the other tasks with so much more ease. In order to overcome laziness, you have to first understand yourself fully, and then use a schedule to capitalize on her strengths.

- **Involve other people**

Studies show that you are likely to honor a commitment when

another person is involved. For instance, if you are supposed to go to the gym at night, just call your best friend and inform them that they will accompany you to the gym. You are less likely to back out simply because you have a relationship going and that you understand each other. Always learn to involve others as it will increase your people skills. Learning to coexist with other human beings is an incredible ability that improves a person's survival skills. Ultimately, involving other people in your affairs may or may not be of help, but it ultimately helps you overcome laziness.

- **Get up from bed**

You know in this present era of technological advancement, there are so many people who are making a nice income working from home. But these people will be the first to admit that laziness is a major issue. But then how would you expect to fight away laziness if you are sprawled on a bed with a magazine to your side? If you want to get rid of laziness at least ensure that you stay away from beds.

- **Dress up**

Fashion psychologists believe that when we dress up, we tend to behave like the character our clothes make us out to be. This can be a bit overwhelming at first. But as time moves, you learn to adjust accordingly. It doesn't matter that you work from home. Whenever laziness comes around, just put on official clothes and look like an executive; the laziness should go.

- **Start the day with a cold shower**

It sounds like an extreme challenge, but there's nothing hard about that. Get into the habit of taking cold showers, and it will help you have improved focus and mental clarity. This will discourage your chances of being lazy. Also, your tendency of taking cold showers should help you cultivate the right mindset so that you are in a position to overcome every last one of your challenges, including laziness.

- **Lift weights**

If you find yourself wanting to curl into a little ball and staying clear of all work, you may remedy the situation by lifting weights. Not exactly bodybuilding, but just lifting weights as if to actually check your system is working. Such tendencies are effective in the long run in helping you achieve the success mindset and overcoming laziness.

- **Write your tasks down**

Instead of keeping all the unfinished tasks in your mind, make a point of writing them down. Writing your tasks down will give you the impetus to confront them head-on. Also, ensure that you make them as detailed as possible. Apart from helping you overcome your laziness, writing your tasks down will also increase your organization skills, and help you become better at managing your affairs.

- **Seek professional help**

If your laziness proves to be getting out of hand, now it's time to meet a doctor. They might check you up to ascertain whether you are all right. And then the next thing they will scan you for various illnesses. It is upon the doctor to decide whether there are some underlying conditions responsible for laziness. Depending on what the doctor finds, they may prescribe drugs, or ask you to perform certain activities. Seeking professional help might seem like a wild idea, but it is very much feasible. Laziness is a terrible thing because it holds you back from making a positive impact in the world, and the consequences may be far too nasty.

- **Eliminate distractions**

Have you ever tried to concentrate when the TV was on? It is usually a frustrating thing to do. The noises and the flashing images keep you from concentrating on the task at hand. And this leads to poor results. Thus, you have to get rid of distractions so that you may tackle your assignments with much zeal. Distractions not only make you lazy, but they also affect your capacity to produce something of superior quality.

- **Have the big picture in mind**

Never lose sight of the big picture. Have it somewhere in your mind's eye, so that whenever you are lazy, you may realize how unfair you are to yourself, and hopefully, you will come back to the right path. The big picture is simply your overriding desire; the father of your goals; what you want to be known for; your lasting legacy!

EMOTIONAL INTELLIGENCE IN LEADERSHIP

A LEADER IS AMONG THE PEOPLE THAT HAVE THE MOST NEED for emotional intelligence. A leader is in a position of authority. And they have to run their affairs in a transparent manner and yet unite their subjects and win the respect of peers. Being a leader is, without a doubt, a tall order. Here are some of the ways that emotionally intelligent leaders manifest their expertise.

- **They have respect for their employees**

Emotionally intelligent leaders don't treat their employees like beggars. Instead, they have the utmost respect for them. They understand too well that these people have played a critical role in helping them sale the heights of success. Leaders who take advantage of their employees and mistreat them usually pay a heavy price. For instance, their top talents tend to migrate into rival organizations at the most inopportune time, leaving their abusive leader disgruntled.

- **They are generous**

Not being generous in the sense of throwing cash away but rather they keep an eye on the performance of their employees, and they can offer best performing employees bonuses. Nothing pains an employee more than seeing that their extremely hard work nets the company so much money, but they are still paid peanuts. So, when a leader comes along who is well aware of this problem, they have no problem rewarding hard-working employees.

- **They build trust between teams and customers**

Emotionally intelligent leaders understand that the best way to improve business climate is through creating a sense of unity between the administration, the workers, and the customers. So, the leader will use various channels of communication and establish great relationships with them. It is not an easy task to get people to trust you, but once you have proven yourself many times over, people may start to see you in a positive light. Anyway, the effort that the CEO invests in promoting closeness never goes unrewarded as it promotes customer loyalty.

- **They are humble**

Some people imagine that simply because you have scaled the heights of success that it is not necessary to be humble. They are obviously wrong about that. Even the good book says that the more you go higher, the more humble you must become. A humble leader is someone that admits when they have done a mistake, and they don't try to shift it to someone else. They are aware that life is about helping one another regardless of the position that the next person occupies. Emotionally intelligent people won't hesitate to help people as long as the mere act won't take away from them.

- **They seek knowledge**

A leader should be someone that seems to have all the answers. No question should be too big for them. But that ability doesn't come through watching TV endlessly and laughing the night away in some dingy bar. Such knowledge comes through reading extensively. Thus, a good leader must set time aside that is meant for study. In this way, they will have great insight into managing their subjects, and also improving their personal finances, as well as the financial status of the organ that they run.

- **They are passionate**

Emotionally intelligent leaders light up when their main interest is mentioned. This indicates that they are passionate about their job. They could talk ceaselessly about their job. It is this attitude that ensures they stick to delivering great leadership and steering both themselves and their subjects forward.

- **They are courageous**

Considering what the world is like, leaders ought to be courageous or else whatever they are representing will be eaten life. They need to be courageous for the purpose of protecting the interests of their subjects, dependents, and customers. They also need to be courageous for the purpose of taking business risks and advancing the cause.

- **They have great listening skills**

Emotionally intelligent people are great at listening to what their juniors are saying. This is also a mark of respect. They don't have to listen to them. Or they may summon just one of them and ask for a summary. But it takes a great and down to earth leader to mix with his employees and listen to them. They employ active listening skill; eye contact, erect posture, and mirroring. They know that they must listen to their employees in order to make sure that the company is running smoothly.

- **They promote teamwork**

Emotionally intelligent leaders understand that although various employees might individually have outstanding ideas, it takes a joint effort to come up with something that is truly revolutionary. Thus, they encourage their employees to join hands and work as a team instead of secluding themselves. Great leaders may split their employees into groups and offer various incentives that will boost their productivity and increase their chances of coming up with innovative ideas.

- **They don't take bribes**

Emotionally intelligent leaders know too well that it is cheap people who would accept bribes in order to be compromised. They consider it beneath them. They will always stand for integrity, which means they will never take bribes. They recognize that giving and taking bribes is the genesis of problems that most private and public entities grapple with, and ultimately, the results are always nasty.

- **They are not economical with "Thank you."**

Emotionally intelligent leaders are every bit as human as everyone else. It's just that they have authority. But what happens when someone does them a favor? Completes a request? They tell that person "Thank you" because that's the right thing to say. It shows that emotionally intelligent leaders are humble and grounded.

- **They are interested in more than academic papers**

Emotionally intelligent people know too well that success is not down to straight A's alone. They know that being able to connect with people is a major skill that is far important than academic papers. They know too well that most people have focused on the academic side and allowed their other capabilities to be dwarfed, so when they run into an exception, they are taken aback. Emotionally intelligent leaders will always be interested in knowing the full range of a person's capabilities to find out if there's a capability of theirs that they can capitalize on.

- **They are not afraid of criticism**

Emotionally intelligent people are not afraid of being criticized. They realize that people will always have something to say about their organization or about them as a person. And so, they welcome constructive criticism and tolerate negative criticism. They have a tough skin, and it is not easy to get to them. Emotionally intelligent leaders never ignore genuine concerns. If they discover that there's an area that seriously needs a remedy, they will be more than obliging to remedy it.

- **They make their words true**

They recognize that their position of power gives them a huge responsibility, and so many people look up to them. The worst that could possibly happen is deceit, especially on their part. And that's why these people ensure that they keep their word. Also, keeping promises makes people have trust in them.

- **They keep their meetings agenda-based**

Emotionally intelligent leaders know too well holding a meeting in which they have nothing important to discover is just a needless waste of time. The leader understands that their biggest resource is time. And they cannot afford to waste their time with reckless abandon. Thus, the leader is interested in calling meetings where he knows of the specific things to talk about as opposed to just swinging in chairs, smiling at each other and then calling the meeting off.

- **They have a system of collecting feedback**

An emotionally intelligent leader may have tough skin, but this is not to mean that they are not sensitive to the needs of their employees or customers. They care to know how their policies are affecting both employees and customers. If they discover that their policies are somewhat oppressive, they will have no qualms about removing those policies. These leaders put systems in place for collecting the necessary feedback.

- **They are great at prioritizing**

Their companies might be involved in a number of things, but still, they will know what is the most important and the least important item, and they will push for the most important item to be given first priority. This indicates a deep awareness of the operations of the company. Also, the tendency to prioritize things is indicative of their calculative personality, which is always a great thing in a leader. A great leader is always cooking up strategies of dominating the market, not just one who settles into generic punches and kicks and gets away hoping that nothing's broken.

- **They are not scared of failure**

Emotionally intelligent leaders are not scared of failure. This is first because they have been through failure before, so it doesn't faze them. Actually, they are not afraid of taking risks that might mean failure, because they know too well that the path to success is littered with failures – both small and large – and it's merely the reaction that seals the deal. But just because they are unafraid of failure doesn't mean they go flinging themselves about, daring fate. By no means!

- **They groom someone to take over**

Emotionally intelligent people think in terms of long term, not short term. They are well aware that one day they won't be around. So what happens to their baby? That's the reason why leaders must groom someone who will ideally take over after them. Emotionally intelligent leaders understand that these positions are transitory. But then they can ensure there diligence is prolonged by mentoring someone to take over.

- **They know their capabilities and their limits**

Emotionally intelligent leaders are well grounded. Their heads aren't bobbing in the clouds. And for that reason, they are realistic about what they can achieve, and at the same time, they are aware of what is beyond their potential. Such honesty with oneself saves a lot of time and energy.

EMOTIONAL INTELLIGENCE FAQ

WHAT IS EMOTIONAL INTELLIGENCE?

It is an individual's capacity to understand and control their emotions, and their capability to start positive interpersonal relationships.

- **In a business setting, which is more important for making sales: EQ or IQ?**

When starting a business, you need to have sufficient IQ to ensure that your systems are working. But then when it comes to making sales, EQ is far more important. This is because you are selling to people, but these people have to feel an emotional connection with you first before they give you their money. People who have poor emotional intelligence have a rough time connecting with customers as their personalities are kind of robotic. But someone with a high level of emotional intelligence will have a great time establishing rapporteur with customers and making the sales pitch. Sales managers are actually equipped with great interpersonal skills that they flash out when talking to customers, and it helps them generate a lot of revenue.

- **Is EI based on manipulation?**

It depends on what angle you are looking from. If you are someone that benefits off of EI, you might not readily admit that it is a manipulative tool. Objectively, emotional intelligence appears to be a discipline that has been there for so long, except we hadn't discipline a suitable phrase for it. People have always grown a soft spot for the charismatic individual that makes a good job of attracting them as opposed to the stammering dweeb that won't say one coherent sentence.

- **What are some of the indications you might have a high emotional intelligence?**

1. Complex emotional vocabulary: the average person expresses their emotional states as either good or bad. But then an emotionally intelligent person uses complex emotional vocabulary that allows him to express a range of emotional statuses. Some of the words that a person with high emotional intelligence might use include: "frustrated" "anxious" "enraged" etc. They can perceive many different emotions.

2. You are really curious: if you have high emotional intelligence, people may have told you many times to stop being so curious about what they are up to. The questions keep coming. Also, emotionally intelligent people seem to be particularly curious about people. This fascination with people stems from a mix of curiosity and their sense of adventure.

3. You embrace change: emotionally unintelligent people are against any form of change. But then emotionally intelligent people are flexible enough to allow changes. Emotionally intelligent people are welcoming to change as they recognize it to be a factor of life that you'd never run away from.

4. You know your strengths and weaknesses: as an emotionally intelligent person, you are well aware of what you are capable of doing brilliantly and what you cannot do at all. This awareness saves you a lot of pain and embarrassment. Knowing your strengths, you can actually capitalize on them and create the best possible life.

5. You're good at reading people: not to say that you possess refined intuitive gifts, but that you are really good at observing people, and realizing you can tell what they really are like out of a very small interaction. For that reason, you are damn great at reading minds.

6. You have thick skin: most emotionally intelligent people tend to have high self-confidence, and they also have an open mind. And so these traits help them in developing a thick skin that hardly ever gets torn. Ordinarily, telling someone that you have something to do may make them feel insulted, and they may label you terrible insults. But then the emotionally intelligent person still won't be fazed.

7. You have no qualms about saying "No": for the most part, you are into doing stuff that will make you feel great about yourself. And for that reason, you find yourself saying "No" to a lot of time wasters and clueless people.

8. You forgive: people with high emotional intelligence tend to

forgive pretty fast. As long as the offender hasn't gone beyond the beyond, then they'll receive forgiveness.

9. You let go of mistakes: emotionally intelligent people make sure that they are not imprisoned by their mistakes. They are interested in keeping a clean heart, and for that reason, they never allow mistakes to bog them down.

10. You give without expecting anything back: that's quite rare. Most people give with strings attached. But then an emotionally intelligent person values experiences more than material acquisitions. This is not to mean they don't care about making progress in life but rather that they are interested in making people happy first and foremost.

11. You don't seek perfection: emotionally intelligent people understand that being a human being, you are prone to errors. Thus, they don't hold themselves to impossible standards. They never seek perfection. And this mentality puts them in a position of power.

12. You are grateful: emotional intelligent people are very thankful for what they have. They know that it takes gratitude to gain even more. And because of their gratitude, they don't have a hard time helping those who are in need, as they understand that the easiest way to receive is through giving.

13. You hate negative self-talk: an emotionally intelligent person hates having to talk negatively about themselves. They know that they are enough and they don't have to talk negatively about themselves. Negative self-talk is in the domain of those people with low emotional intelligence.

14. You won't give anyone the power to deny you happiness: emotionally intelligent people value their happiness so much.

Thus, they won't tolerate having someone sneak up on them and try to rob them of their happiness.

- **Why is emotional intelligence significant?**

1. Self-awareness: through emotional intelligence, you can finally understand your emotional makeup. You can identify the various emotions that you feel. And you can understand your emotional needs.

2. Emotional regulation: sometimes you may experience raw emotions and feel a deep urge to explode, but the emotional intelligence teaches us to keep our raw emotions in check and let them out in an acceptable, non-confrontational manner.

3. Empathy: emotional intelligence promotes a skill known as empathy amongst warriors. It is basically the capacity of an individual to wear the shoes of another person who is going through a turbulent moment.

4. Social skills: emotional intelligence puts an emphasis on developing social skills. At the heart of emotional intelligence is the promotion of person-to-person interaction. And for that reason, it is incredibly important to have skills for interacting with other people.

CPSIA information can be obtained
at www.ICGtesting.com
Printed in the USA
LVHW020322280720
661718LV00018B/1208